JUST EAT

PURE *and* SIMPLE COOKING

RENATE A. MOORE

Terri + Glenn

Happy Cooking ♡

[signature]

10/28/23

SPARK Publications

Charlotte, North Carolina

JUST EAT

PURE *and* SIMPLE COOKING

Renate A. Moore

Designed, produced, and published by SPARK Publications
SPARKpublications.com
Charlotte, NC

Photography by Mark Santo
except stock image on page 116

Printed in the United States of America
Hardcover, March 2019, ISBN: 978-1-943070-51-0
Full-Color Softcover, March 2019, ISBN: 978-1-943070-52-7
Black & White Softcover, March 2019, ISBN: 978-1-943070-54-1
E-book, March 2019, ISBN: 978-1-943070-53-4
Library of Congress Control Number: 2019931241

COOKING / Regional & Ethnic / Central American & South American
COOKING / Regional & Ethnic / American / Southern States
COOKING / Comfort Food

just eat • dedication

DEDICATION

For my wonderful mother, Sheila, who is as fiery and beautiful as she was twenty years ago. Thinking back that far makes me realize that I can't even begin to imagine what life would be like without her. She's always been a constant source of inspiration and unconditional support. She always encouraged me to be ambitious and fearless. Plus I have her to thank for many of what I like to think are my best personality traits—from fashion to cooking to being a strong yet humble, independent woman who is not afraid to take risks while making a positive impact by helping others.

I will never forget the words that my mom said to me when I was a teenager as she taught me to iron a shirt. "In life never let anything rule you—you rule it," she said. I was circling around the ironing board trying to master this lesson. She took the shirt, shook it out, and showed me how to iron it without moving around the board. Anytime I feel challenged, I reflect on what she told me that day.

just eat

TABLE OF CONTENTS

ethnic & traditional

renate's spin

breakfast delights

soups

desserts

holiday classics

party favs

sips

dips

this & that

FOREWORD

You are in for a tasty treat, dear reader. Beyond the scrumptious recipes Renate will share with you on the following pages, you will experience Renate's delicious stories from her childhood in Guyana, South America, to her present as proprietor of Lady Ren's Bakery and Books—all shared with you through food.

I've been eager for Renate's memoir of recipes since I first learned of her project. Working with Renate, or "Lady Ren," has been such a joy. We resonate. I suppose it should come as no surprise: my background is in library science, and Renate is an author with a librarian background. We didn't meet in the library world, however. We came together as Baker Supreme (my words) and Tea Lady.

From the first, Renate's skill in the kitchen and her food philosophy (which, simply put, is wholesome goodness), her integrity in life and doing business, and her indomitable personality impressed me and drew me in. We have collaborated on several joint ventures, and we're always pairing Lady Ren's baked delights with KTeas' thoughtfully curated teas.

Over time, Renate and I grew beyond business associates and became strong friends. You can imagine, then, that I was thrilled and honored when Renate approached me on yet another collaboration—when she asked me to write this foreword to her recipe memoir. The glimpse above of the person who created this recipe book is not all I have to offer you as enticement to read on.

What I love the most about this memoir Renate has put together is that she imbues it with a sense of hearth and home, with the warmth and generosity of her spirit—as if Renate has invited you into her kitchen, and while you prepare these meals together, she regales you with stories from her life's journey. There's vibrancy in Renate's cooking, a reliance on fresh, pure, and simple ingredients that I know will be appealing to everyone who uses her book. Renate's love for fresh and healthy is evident throughout these pages.

Enjoy reading, enjoy cooking and eating, and enjoy making your own memories and traditions.

Kathryn Isaacs
KTeas Specialty Teas and Gifts
2019

just eat

INTRODUCTION

We are living in an era of food confusion. Terms like vegan, primal, and gluten-free seem to accompany a fear of eating, especially sweets and desserts. I constantly hear people say they don't know what to eat and they are confused about how to "eat right." With so many competing theories on nutrition fighting for our attention, no wonder people are confused. I find myself telling friends and family, "Just eat!" when they struggle over whether to eat a dessert or a meal. I remind them to think about all those who gave up dessert the night the Titanic sank. Food is not the enemy! I hope this cookbook will help you overcome food confusion.

Growing up, I spent a lot of time helping my mom prepare traditional foods that were part of our lifestyle. I am an Indo-Guyanese American girl originally from Guyana, a sovereign state on the northern mainland of South America. Originally inhabited by many indigenous groups, Guyana was settled by the Dutch before coming under the British Empire in the late eighteenth century. It was governed as British Guiana, with mostly a plantation-style economy until the 1950s. It gained independence in 1966 and officially became a republic within the Commonwealth of Nations in 1970. The legacy of British rule is reflected in the country's political administration and diverse population, which includes Indian, African, Amerindian, and multiracial groups.

Stuffed (Deviled) Eggs (pg. 97)

In Guyana, festivities constantly surrounded me. Weddings lasted for a week with celebrations and cooking every day. Music, dancing, and sometimes arguments that were hysterical to watch were the norm in my young life. In all the stories I've heard of my ancestors, my family has been about retaining a network of love and compassion. With compassion comes comfort and with comfort comes food. Food, the kitchen, and cooking together were the centerpiece of family tradition, which subtly and not-so-subtly encouraged us to face our emotions together. We seemed to gather in the kitchen no matter the occasion. We enjoyed food and all the memories we'd made whether they were trial or tribulation.

A lot of dishes I make today remind me of something in my childhood—some nostalgic

Shrimp Bok Choy (pg 31)

memory of large, loud crowds of family at my grandparents' estate filled with a variety of exotic fruit trees and flower gardens. Although cooking was more of a chore, the harmony of the times around meals grew on me in such a way that when I was finally on my own, it had transformed into one of my deepest loves.

When I moved away from home and migrated to the United States, I quickly realized I was in charge of making my own meals. It was also apparent that without my mom's direction, it was challenging to replicate the traditional foods I grew up eating. So I started practicing and playing around with recipes and asking my mom over phone conversations how to cook some of the nostalgic foods I love. With practice, I became an expert at making these foods that I now make for my family and friends.

I did not start out my career as a gourmet baker and writer, but I find it quite interesting that food led me to where I am now. I had worked in the real estate, finance, and international education industries. When a job relocation brought my husband, children, and me from New York to North Carolina, excitement and high expectations turned into unhappiness and disappointment. I endured many challenges of getting acclimated and finding a job. After a while, I decided to turn those challenges around by bringing to life what I was saving for retirement—owning a café and bookstore that would enable people to eat better and stimulate their minds to live their best. With a little cash and my passion for cooking and writing, I applied my skills and knowledge to create my own business, Lady Ren's Bakery & Books. I make desserts with all-natural and organic ingredients and write to encourage reading.

People may consider me a foodie and a critic, but that's far from the truth. I haven't attended culinary school or traveled the world seeking new food experiences. I'm neither a dietician nor a nutritionist, nor am I certified to provide medical advice or meal plans. I'm simply a woman who enjoys good food. But—yes, there is always a "but"—I also know we must enjoy food with balance and moderation while paying attention to what and how much we eat.

It's true that food is necessary for survival, but it is also an experience to be savored and not condemned. Allow yourself to enjoy life and taste how amazing properly fueling your body can be. The key points to enjoying food, including dessert, is to pay attention to the ingredients. Stay away from artificial ingredients and preservatives as much as you can.

I believe that food is a highly personal choice. It's cultural, emotional, social, political, and health-related. You are the only one who can make the best possible decision for your body and your life.

That being said, the way I grew up eating is what I continue to practice. We ate a mix of all-natural, whole foods focusing on fresh vegetables, lean protein, whole grains, and sweets. But we ate in moderation, and we stayed active. A well-balanced mix can provide a full range of vitamins and minerals while being deliciously satisfying. Experiment and discover what you like.

I want to share some of my favorite family meals with you in this cookbook in hopes the easy-to-follow recipes will make *cooking* them as fun and delightful as *eating* them. I recommend using these recipes as a guide and customizing to suit your tastes like I did. Or you can follow the recipe exactly until you have learned the method of making the dish. We all have a different preference for seasonings and ingredients. My ultimate goal is to encourage and inspire you to connect with food and learn about the ingredients and flavors of South American cuisine with a fusion of exquisite North American dishes, no matter which method you choose.

The recipes in this book range from ethnic, traditional, and sentimental to my twist on modern and fun. I'm inspired by all ingredients and how to use them in unique ways while keeping a focus on classic dishes. So whether you're looking for family dinner ideas, holiday classics, or a decadent dessert, you are sure to find them here. My simple and healthy recipes will help you get food on the table fast. They are versatile and can be easily transformed into vegan or vegetarian dishes without compromising flavor.

As you prepare these recipes, I welcome you to experience happiness, home, and many treasured moments together and to live your best life!

Happy Cooking!
Renate

Ginger Refresher (pg 105)

ethnic & traditional

CURRY CHICKEN
SERVES 6

Guyana, South America, is not necessarily the place where you would expect to find curry chicken, yet the diverse population of this small country consists vastly of Indian, African, Amerindian, Chinese, and multiracial groups. Therefore, many traditional Indian dishes are a staple in the Guyanese cuisine. Although each cook uses the same basic yet exotic spices, every dish of curry tastes unique.

For example, you'll notice most of my recipes begin with red and yellow bell peppers and similar spices. This has become my signature because I enjoy these flavors immensely. You may have already acquired your own signature. Feel free to play around with your palette and have fun interchanging ingredients!

3 tablespoons curry powder	3 pounds chicken, cut into medium pieces
1 tablespoon garam masala	3 curry leaves or bay leaves
½ teaspoon ground cumin	1 cinnamon stick
½ teaspoon ground turmeric	5 whole cloves
6 cloves garlic, minced	1 small hot ghost or chili pepper or hot pepper of your choice (optional)
1 tablespoon tomato paste	3 whole potatoes, medium diced
3 tablespoons water	1 to 1½ cups water
4 tablespoons canola oil	2 green onions, sliced medium
1 onion, chopped medium	Salt to taste
¼ of a red bell pepper, diced	
¼ of a yellow bell pepper, diced	

QUICK TIP

A common misconception is that curry is always spicy-hot. You can regulate the intensity by adding a whole hot pepper or a small piece to your liking as indicated in this recipe.

In a small bowl, combine the curry powder, garam masala, cumin, turmeric, minced garlic, tomato paste, and water to form a paste.

On medium flame, heat oil, add the curry paste and stir well. Cover and cook this mixture for about 6 minutes on low heat, stirring often to prevent burning. Add the onions and bell peppers and cook for 2 minutes.

Add the chicken, sprinkle with salt, and mix well to combine the curry paste. Add the curry or bay leaves, cinnamon stick, cloves and hot pepper. Cover and let simmer for about 20 minutes, stirring a few times.

Add the potatoes and 1 to 1½ cups water (enough water to cook the potatoes and provide a gravy). Cook for an additional 20 minutes or until potatoes and chicken are tender and fully cooked. Add the green onions.

Taste for flavor. Add more salt if needed.

Remove and discard the cinnamon stick, cloves, and bay leaves. Serve and enjoy with cooked white basmati or jasmine rice and a side garden salad.

RED SNAPPER WITH CURRY SAUCE
SERVES 4

Do you have some eaters who are fishy about fish? This recipe will be the catch of the day. The zest of the spices and method of concocting this meal distracts the pickiest of taste buds, inviting a new relationship with this nutrient-enriched protein source. After prepping, the cook time is, at most, 35 minutes making it an ideal after-work meal. I suggest prepping in the morning and throwing it all together for dinner time. Your taste testers will assume you snuck by your local Indian restaurant or think you've been working at it all day.

4	large red snapper fillets
1	lemon, juiced
1	cup water, room temperature
1	tablespoon tomato paste
2	tablespoons curry powder
½	teaspoon garam masala
½	teaspoon ground cumin
1	teaspoon ground turmeric
1	tablespoon water
2	tablespoons olive oil

6	cloves garlic, minced
1	medium sweet onion, sliced thinly (julienne-style)
1	celery stalk, sliced thinly (julienne-style)
1	(16 oz.) can coconut milk
2	bay leaves or curry leaves
1	large tomato, seeded and sliced thinly (julienne-style)
2	cups cooked jasmine or basmati white rice

QUICK TIP

"Julienne" is a method of slicing fruits, vegetables, and meats into strips that resemble matchsticks. Julienne strips are often used in stir-fries. They are also used as a decorative cut to garnish various dishes.

In a baking dish, give the fish a lemon bath by mixing the lemon juice and water, add the fillets, and marinate for 3 minutes. Then rinse and drain.

In a small bowl, combine the tomato paste, curry powder, garam masala, cumin, turmeric, and 1 tablespoon water.

In a deep pot, heat the oil on medium, then stir in curry mixture and cook for 5 minutes. Add the garlic, onion, and celery and cook for 10 minutes, stirring often.

Add the coconut milk and bay or curry leaves. Bring to a boil, then simmer on low for 12 minutes, stirring occasionally.

Add the sliced tomatoes and the fillets skin side up gently covering them with the sauce. Simmer for 8 to 10 minutes or until the fish is cooked through and flakes easily with a fork.

Transfer the fillets to a warm serving dish and cover to keep warm. Continue to simmer the sauce until it reaches the desired consistency. Remove and discard bay or curry leaves and ladle the sauce over the fillets. Serve hot with cooked rice.

LYENNIE'S FRIED RICE
SERVES 6 TO 8

Aunt Lyennie was the quintessential beacon of love and affection for me throughout my life making this plate near and dear to my heart. Fried rice is another staple dish for family gatherings in Guyana, and simply put, Aunt Lyennie's was the best. Her attentiveness to fried rice was synonymous to the time she spent with me—always giving and always fully present. The aroma lights up the senses, just as my Aunt Lyennie would light up the room. Hands down, this will be one of the best-loved and most requested meals! As my husband says, "This one calls for a repeat."

4   pieces boneless or bone-in chicken thighs, cut into thin pieces*

3   cloves garlic, minced

3   teaspoons adobo all-purpose seasoning

1   teaspoon sweet paprika

1   teaspoon Worcestershire sauce

4   teaspoons soy sauce, divided

1   teaspoon fresh grated ginger or 1 teaspoon ground ginger

1   teaspoon fresh thyme, finely chopped

1   teaspoon sesame oil

2   cups uncooked, whole grain basmati rice

3   cups water

1   chicken bouillon cube

2   teaspoons salt

5   tablespoons canola oil, divided

2   tablespoons olive oil

½   cup fresh green beans or long beans, thinly sliced

½   red bell pepper, medium chopped

½   yellow bell pepper, medium chopped

4–5 teaspoons ground star anise

3   tablespoons oyster sauce

2   celery stalks with leaves, medium chopped, save leaves for garnishing

1   medium carrot, thinly shredded

1   cup baby corn or 15 oz. can sweet whole kernel corn (drained)

3   green onions, finely sliced

Fresh-ground black pepper (optional)

¼   cup chopped parsley

*If using bone-in thighs, slice the meat small and leave the bone for flavor. Substitute chicken with meat of your choice or use shrimp instead. This recipe can also be prepared as a vegetarian dish by omitting the meats.

Marinate the meat: Place the chicken in a medium bowl. Add the garlic, 2 teaspoons adobo, sweet paprika, Worcestershire sauce, 3 teaspoons soy sauce, grated fresh ginger, and chopped thyme. Cover and refrigerate overnight or marinate for 1 hour before cooking.

Steam the rice: Place a large pot on medium flame and heat 1 teaspoon sesame oil. Rinse, drain, and add the rice to the sesame oil and toast for about 1 minute. Then carefully add the water, bouillon, and salt. Turn the flame down to very low and steam the rice until the water is absorbed, about 15 minutes. Empty the cooked rice into a large bowl to cool, drizzle with 2 tablespoons canola oil, and stir. This prevents the rice from clumping together.

Cook the meat: Place olive oil in a skillet, add marinated chicken, and cook until brown, about 8–10 minutes. Turn the flame off and stir in the chopped bell peppers and green or long beans.

Mix the rice: To the cooled rice, add the ground anise, oyster sauce, 1 teaspoon soy sauce, and 1 teaspoon adobo in small increments, stirring, tasting for flavor, and adding more until you have the level of flavor you like. Add in the cooked meat and vegetables (except green onions and chopped parsley or celery leaves), grated carrots and corn and mix well. Add fresh-ground black pepper (to taste) and stir.

Stir-fry. In the same pot where you cooked the rice, heat 3 tablespoons canola oil. Add the rice mixture and stir-fry for about 4 minutes. Taste again for desired flavor, adding more salt or ground black pepper or oyster sauce if needed. Turn off the flame and sprinkle the chopped parsley and/or celery leaves and green onions over the rice. When ready to serve, stir the dish once more to mix in the chopped herbs.

Serve warm.

just eat • *ethnic & traditional*

LO MEIN SOUTH AMERICAN STYLE
SERVES 6 TO 8

This is one of several staple meals we served at family gatherings. In retrospect, I can see it was a sneaky way to get us to eat our vegetables. This dish brings back childhood memories of spending summer holidays with cousins and how I did not like the texture of green onions. (In Guyana, we called green onions "shallots" and never had actual shallots.)

When we gathered to eat, it took me a long time to finish because I would pick out all of the onions and place them around my plate. My cousins would look at me with disgust. I can still picture their faces every time I make this dish, and we laugh about it now when we reflect on our childhood days. It wasn't until I was older that I slowly started to stop decorating my plate with green onions. Funny enough, I learned that the flavor of the green onions makes this dish impeccable. Now, green onions are an important part of my summer kitchen garden.

4   pieces boneless or bone-in chicken thighs, washed and cut into thin pieces

3   cloves garlic, minced

3   teaspoons adobo all-purpose seasoning, divided

1   teaspoon Worcestershire sauce

4   teaspoons soy sauce, divided

1   teaspoon fresh thyme, finely chopped

1   teaspoon sweet paprika

1   teaspoon fresh grated ginger or 1 teaspoon ground ginger

Dash of fresh-ground black pepper (optional)

Water for cooking noodles

Dash of salt

5   tablespoons canola oil, divided

16 oz. packet of lo mein noodles (spaghetti noodles can be substituted)

½   cup frozen green peas

1   cup broccoli crowns, whole

½   cup fresh green beans, chopped small

2   tablespoons olive oil

4–5 teaspoons ground star anise

3   tablespoons oyster sauce

½   red bell pepper, medium chopped

½   yellow bell pepper, medium chopped

2   celery stalks with leaves, medium chopped, save leaves for garnishing

1   medium carrot, thinly shredded

1   cup baby corn or 1 (15-ounce) can of sweet whole kernel corn (drained)

2   blades of scallions (or green onions), chopped small

Salt to taste

Marinate chicken with minced garlic, 2 teaspoons adobo seasoning, Worcestershire sauce, 2 teaspoons soy sauce, finely chopped thyme, sweet paprika, ginger, and a dash of ground black pepper. Cover and refrigerate overnight or 1 hour before cooking.

Fill a large pot with water to cook the noodles. Add a dash of salt and 1 tablespoon canola oil. When the water is boiling rapidly, carefully add the noodles and cook for 7 to 8 minutes. Then add the frozen peas, broccoli crowns, and green beans and blanch for 1 minute. Drain well then place in a large bowl with 1 tablespoon canola oil. Stir and let cool.

Heat the olive oil in a skillet, add the marinated chicken, and cook until brown, about 8 to 10 minutes.

To the noodles, add the ground anise, oyster sauce, 2 teaspoons soy sauce, and 1 teaspoon adobo in small increments, stirring until incorporated, tasting for flavor, and adding a little more until you have the level of savory you like. Add in chopped peppers, chopped celery stalks, grated carrots, and corn and then mix well. Add the meat and mix well to combine.

Using the same pot where you boiled the noodles, heat 3 tablespoons canola oil, then toss in the mixed noodles. Stir-fry for about 4 minutes, then turn off the flame. Sprinkle the chopped green onions, parsley, and/or celery leaves on top. When ready to serve, stir once more to mix in the chopped leaves.

Serve warm.

RENATE'S PEAS & RICE

SERVES 4 TO 6

1 cup dried pigeon peas or red kidney beans, soaked overnight*

Dash of salt

Water to cook the beans

2 cloves garlic, minced

½ yellow sweet onion, medium chopped

¼ cup red bell pepper, chopped

¼ cup yellow bell pepper, medium chopped

½ cup unsweetened coconut milk

½ cup chicken, beef, or vegetable stock

3 green onions, thinly sliced diagonally

3 sprigs fresh thyme

1½ cups long-grain rice (uncooked but rinsed and drained)

Salt and pepper to taste

Fresh parsley leaves finely chopped, for garnish

1 scotch bonnet pepper, seeds and membrane removed and chopped (optional)**

Drain the beans and place in a medium pot with a little salt, then cover with water. Bring to a simmer and cook until the beans are tender, about 1 to 1½ hours.

In a small sauté pan, add the garlic, onion, and bell peppers and cook for 3 minutes.

When the beans are tender, stir in the sautéed peppers and onions, then add coconut milk, stock, green onions, and thyme. Raise the heat to a boil. Stir in the rice and add salt and pepper. (If you like spicy-hot flavor, see notes below for how to add some heat.)

Cover the pot and turn the heat down to very low. Cook until the rice is tender and has absorbed most of the liquid.

Taste for seasoning, adding more salt and pepper if needed. Replace the lid and cook until all of the liquid is absorbed and the rice is tender (not too soft).

When ready to serve, transfer to a large serving bowl.

*I love pigeon peas, so that is always my first choice. If you don't have dried pigeon peas on hand, you can substitute with a can of pigeon peas, drained and rinsed, then added when the liquids are absorbed in the rice.

**If you like hot-flavored foods, you can add 1 scotch bonnet pepper to simmer while the rice cooks. Note: when handling the hot pepper, be careful not to touch your eyes or face. I suggest wearing a food glove while handling the pepper and thoroughly wash your cutting board and any utensils that touched the pepper once you are done

FEARLESS FRIED OKRA & SHRIMP

SERVES 4 TO 6

Living in North Carolina now, I witness firsthand the love for my favorite vegetable: okra! Although this veggie is served in many countries across the world, it's still quiet a mystery to many people. The biggest nose-turner that I hear around okra is its slimy texture. Tending to our family garden as a child, I became very fond and familiar with this unique veg, and the way it had always been prepared for me was an easy, eloquent, and most importantly, *slimeless* display. It's OK to have fear; I'll help you through that with this easy recipe.

2 pounds fresh okra	1 pound shrimp (frozen or fresh washed, cleaned and deveined)
½ cup canola or vegetable oil	¼ teaspoon adobo all-purpose seasoning
½ medium size sweet yellow onion, chopped small	¼ teaspoon fresh lemon juice
3 garlic cloves, peeled and minced	½ teaspoon salt
¼ cup red bell peppers, diced	1 green onion, diced
¼ cup yellow bell peppers, diced	
1 Roma tomato, diced	

QUICK TIP

A gelatinous solution called mucilage *is found in okra pods. Made of sugar residues and proteins, mucilage's viscosity increases when heat is applied. This is good for thickening dishes but bad if you're trying to sauté sliced okra. If you skip air drying the okra, when you cook them, they will become soggy and mushy because of the fluid. (Hence, the slime.)*

Rinse and dry the okra thoroughly. Slice into ¼ inch thickness for a crispier texture. (The thicker you cut them, the softer they will be once cooked).

Spread the chopped okra on a baking sheet and place near a window or sunny area (kitchen table or counter top) and let air dry overnight. The reason for this step is to dry out the "slimy" texture inside the okra.

Once the okra is dried, you will notice the seeds look slightly brown. This is how you know it is ready to be cooked.

Use a wide-bottomed frying pan or stir-fry pan so that the okra can spread out nicely when being cooked. Heat oil to a medium heat and add the onions, garlic, and peppers. Cook until tender (about 3 minutes). Add the tomatoes and shrimp. Sprinkle with adobo all-purpose seasoning and cook for 2 minutes. (Do not overcook the shrimp). Remove the shrimp and place in a bowl and set aside.

To the same pan, add the okra and turn continuously for a few minutes. Turn the heat to low. Add the lemon juice, cover, and cook for 5 to 7 minutes.

Remove the lid, stir the okra, and add ½ teaspoon salt. It is important not to add the salt too early in the process because you can risk the okra becoming mushy as salt tends to bring out fluids from vegetables. Taste for flavor. If you prefer more salt, sprinkle more to desired flavor.

After adding salt, continuously stir the okra until it starts to shrink in size. If you prefer a softer texture and not as crisp, turn the heat off before they start to turn dark brown. If you prefer them crispier then continue to cook a little longer. Add the cooked shrimp and diced green onions. Stir and cook for 1 minute, then remove from the heat.

Enjoy with cooked basmati rice or roti.

ROTI

MAKES 8 TO 10

This bread is popular in Caribbean cuisine, and there are many different ways of making it. None are better than the other; there are just different methods of achieving your preference. Roti was the first dish I learned to cook when I was seven years old. I learned from my mother how to make it by being in the kitchen with her and following her directions. Her key to successful roti relies more on technique than the quality of ingredients. Not over kneading the dough, using the right temperature of water, allowing the dough to rest, creating enough layers for air pockets when oiling and rolling it up into dough balls, and ensuring the roti has been "clapped" while hot are the measures she uses to ensure a great roti.

"Clapping" is a Guyanese term used to describe the method of releasing air pockets from the roti. Once the roti is done cooking, it is tossed up in the air and clapped with both hands repeatedly. (Mom's method is three claps.) This releases the air pockets and creates flakes, but it can be hot to your hands! There are many different methods used today instead of "clapping," including placing the hot roti in two bowls and shaking repeatedly. This method works great for protecting your hands from the heat. My method is to place the hot roti on a sheet of paper towel, fold, and give it three "claps." I prefer this method to using the bowls.

3   cups all-purpose flour, more
    for kneading and dusting
2   teaspoons baking powder
½   teaspoon salt

¼   cup canola or vegetable oil,
    vegetable shortening, or ghee
    (clarified butter), melted
1   cup medium-warm (room temperature)
    water, more as needed
    extra oil for basting and cooking

QUICK TIP

Try not to get too intimidated by preparing roti. Instead, have fun with it, bring the kids or your partner into the process, and relax. The taste will be fine even if the shape or texture isn't quite what you desire. You'll get the hang of it. Get your hands in there! Enjoy the art of cooking.

In a medium bowl, sift the flour, baking powder, and salt together.

Form a well in the mixture, then add the oil (or melted vegetable shortening or ghee) and water a little at a time and knead into a soft, smooth ball. (It will become a sticky dough.)

Add a little more flour until you have a soft texture. Rub a little oil on the top of the dough to prevent crusting. Cover with a kitchen towel or plate. Let dough rest for a minimum of 45 minutes.

Divide the dough into 3-inch balls. Then using a rolling pin, roll out each dough ball into a disc 1/8 inch in thickness. (The disc will be roughly the size and shape of a tortilla.) Brush with oil and lightly sprinkle with flour. Next, use a knife to make a slit across the radius of the circle. Then roll the dough clockwise (right to left) to create a cone. Tuck the end into the center of the cone. The dough should resemble a flat rose. When finished with this step, cover the dough with a kitchen towel and let rest for at least 30 minutes.

Heat a square or round skillet to medium heat. Roll each cone into a dough ball to 1/8-inch thickness to form a nice, flat circle.

Place the roti in the skillet to cook. Once the roti shows tiny bubbles, flip them and brush with oil. Flip back to the first side and brush with oil. Cook for about 20 seconds then remove from heat.

Immediately place roti in a deep bowl, cover with a plate, and shake vigorously to release air pockets in the roti. Alternatively, you may "clap" the roti with your hands, using your bare hands or a paper towel (best method for roti texture).

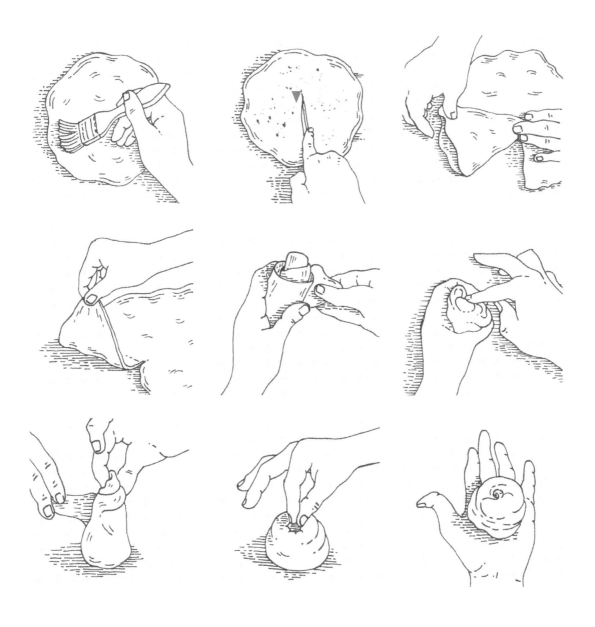

If you're not ready to serve the roti immediately, stack them in a plate, cover with a paper towel, and then wrap with a kitchen towel to maintain soft texture. This can be kept at room temperature up to 6 hours. Then wrap in wax paper and place in a covered container and refrigerate up to 5 days. You can also freeze and reheat them as needed. To reheat, wrap the roti in a moist to wet paper towel and microwave for 1 to 2 minutes, depending on your likeness of heat. The roti will keep its soft texture and not get hard or crisp. It can also be reheated in a toaster oven for 2 minutes or, for crisper texture, 3 minutes.

BAIGAN CHOKA (ROASTED EGGPLANT)

SERVES 4 TO 6

If you visit my house any week of the year, you will smell baigan choka perfuming the air. Although poles apart in taste, baigan choka is similar to baba ghanoush. I'd say the main difference is that baigan choka contains more additions, such as sweet yellow bell peppers, sliced green onions, and a traditional flavorful pepper called wiri-wiri (scotch bonnet pepper is a good substitute) that give it more intensity and refined flavor. It is delicious for any meal, but I prefer it for lunch since lunch is my heartier meal of the day. Traditionally, this menu item is prepared over an open flame while others bake it in the oven or on the grill. I prefer to roast mine the old-fashioned way like my mom did on a gas stove top and following her recipe. Although it is a little more time consuming, I find I get more of a charred taste from roasting over a gas stove or open fire on a grill. Wrapping the eggplant in aluminum foil prevents mess. This is a popular dish in Guyanese cuisine. People have many different ways of making it, so make it your own too! The perfect accompaniment for this course is roti (see recipe on page 26), a bread similar to pita.

2 medium eggplants, rinsed and dried	2 green onions, thinly sliced
4 garlic cloves, peeled and sliced in half	1 teaspoon oil
Salt and pepper to taste	Wiri-wiri or scotch bonnet pepper, finely chopped (optional)
2 tablespoons yellow bell pepper, finely diced	

WHAT IS BAIGAN CHOKA?

A choka is primarily a dish made with vegetables or dry-cured fish, roasted or fire-roasted to impart a unique smoky flavor. Bigan choka is a vegetarian dish prepared by mashing eggplant (baigan) that has been grilled over charcoal or direct fire.

With a kitchen knife, make two slits on the sides of the eggplants, then stuff with sliced garlic cloves. Wrap the eggplants in aluminum foil. Make two handles on the side to help with rotating while roasting. Roast the eggplant for 30 minutes on the burners of stove top over medium high heat or bake in the oven at 400 F until tender.

Once the eggplant is done roasting, open foil, slit down the center, and remove the insides, including the roasted garlic, into a mixing bowl. Mash with a fork to loosen the eggplant.

Add salt and black pepper to suit your tastes. Then stir in the yellow bell pepper and green onions.

Place a small pot over medium heat, then add the oil to heat. Add the eggplant and stir fry for about 4 minutes, then stir in wiri-wiri or scotch bonnet pepper if desired.

Serve hot with pita bread or roti.

EGGPLANT STEW WITH CHICKEN
SERVES 6 TO 8

Solanum melongena, or "eggplant" as we call it in the US, is a fruit in the nightshade family. So despite its gourd-like shape, it's actually more closely related to tomatoes, peppers, and potatoes. In various parts of Europe, it is called "aubergine," which is also the name of the deep purple variety we see most often in stores, although it also grows in shades of yellow and white. Originally cultivated in India, it is known there as "baigan," "baingan," or "brinjal." And because Guyanese cooking is so heavily influenced by Indian cuisine, baigan dishes were common in the meals of my youth.

½ teaspoon salt

½ teaspoon ground black pepper

½ teaspoon paprika

½ teaspoon poultry seasoning

1 teaspoon Worcestershire sauce

1 teaspoon soy sauce

4 skinless, boneless chicken thighs or breasts, medium diced

2 large eggplants (preferably Chinese or Japanese eggplants)

½ of a medium sweet Vidalia onion, diced

1 roma tomato, diced

2 cloves garlic, minced

¼ cup red bell peppers, diced

¼ cup yellow bell peppers, diced

1 celery stalk, diced

2 green onions, sliced

2 medium potatoes, diced into small pieces

2–3 tablespoon olive oil for sautéing

2 tablespoon tomato paste

Salt and pepper to taste

QUICK TIP

This dish can be prepared without meat as a vegetarian dish. Also, shrimp, beef or pork can be substituted for chicken.

In a medium bowl, combine the ½ teaspoon salt, ½ teaspoon ground black pepper, paprika, poultry seasoning, Worcestershire sauce, and soy sauce. Add in the chicken and toss to coat. Let sit for about 15 minutes while you prepare the eggplant.

Fill a bowl with cold, lightly salted water. Trim the stems of the eggplants and discard. Chop each eggplant in half by cutting lengthwise from top to bottom. Cut each half horizontally, then medium dice and place in the bowl of water. Set aside.

Prep other ingredients. Chop the onions, tomato, garlic, bell peppers, and celery. Slice the green onions. Set aside.

Fill another bowl with cold water. Peel and chop the potatoes, then place them in the bowl of cold water. Set aside.

Place the oil in a medium-sized pot and heat on medium-high. Add the diced onions, tomatoes, garlic, bell peppers, and celery. Cook until tender and fragrant, about 3 minutes. Stir in the tomato paste and cook for 1 minute.

Add chicken and stir to combine. Cover and cook about 8 minutes.

Add eggplant, sprinkle with salt and pepper to taste, and stir to combine. Cover and cook for about 20 minutes, then add in the potatoes.

Turn heat to low. Let eggplant cook until tender and potatoes are cooked through. Stir in sliced green onions.

Adjust salt and seasonings to suit your tastes.

OH-SO-EASY CABBAGE STEW
SERVES 6 TO 8

1   pound beef, rinsed thoroughly and cut into cubes (beef for stewing)

2   cloves garlic, minced

2   tablespoons soy sauce

1   teaspoon adobo all-purpose seasoning

½   teaspoon sweet paprika

1   teaspoon Worcestershire sauce

½   teaspoon Tony Chachere's creole seasoning

1   teaspoon fresh thyme, minced (or ½ teaspoon dried thyme)

2   tablespoons canola or vegetable oil

1   tablespoon tomato paste

½   medium sized sweet Vidalia onion, chopped

¼   red bell pepper, chopped

¼   yellow bell pepper, chopped

2   green onions, sliced

1-2 cups water or beef broth for cooking the meat

1   medium green cabbage, washed and cut into thick lengthwise pieces

1   medium tomato, chopped

2   tablespoons fresh parsley, chopped

1   hot pepper (optional)

Salt to taste

QUICK TIP

Cabbage is one of the most inexpensive leafy vegetables yet is loaded with so much nutritional value. Not only is it heart healthy, but also it acts as an anti-inflammatory agent, helps with digestion, and is a good source of fiber and many essential vitamins. Growing up, cabbage was on our menu once a week!

Marinate the beef with minced garlic, soy sauce, adobo seasoning, sweet paprika, Worcestershire sauce, Tony Chachere's seasoning, minced thyme, and any other of your favorite seasonings and dry herbs. Cover and marinate overnight or for 30 minutes before cooking.

In a large pot, heat the oil, then add the tomato paste and cook for 1 minute, stirring frequently to avoid burning. Stir in the chopped sweet onions, bell peppers, and green onions and cook until softened.

Add the beef, stir, cover, and let cook for 5 to 7 minutes. Remove the lid, add 1 cup of water or beef broth, cover and continue to cook the meat until soft and tender, adding more water or broth as needed.

Add the chopped cabbage, tomato, parsley, and hot pepper (if using). Sprinkle with salt, stir, cover, and cook for about 20 minutes. Taste for flavor. Add more salt or pepper if desired.

Serve hot with rice or roti.

SHRIMP BOK-CHOY
SERVES 6

2 tablespoons canola oil

½ sweet yellow onion, medium diced

2 cloves garlic, minced

½ cup red bell pepper, medium diced

½ cup yellow bell pepper, medium diced

6 cherry tomatoes, sliced in halves

½ pound shrimp (deveined, thawed if frozen)

¼ teaspoon adobo all-purpose seasoning

4 heads baby bok choy, washed thoroughly and thinly sliced

½ teaspoon salt, more if desired

2 green onions, sliced

In a large pan, heat the oil on medium and add the yellow onions, garlic, and peppers. Cook until tender (about 3 minutes).

Add the tomatoes and shrimp. Sprinkle with adobo seasoning and cook for 2 minutes. (Do not overcook the shrimp). Remove only the shrimp and place in a bowl and set aside.

To the same pan, add the chopped bok choy and stir for a few minutes. Cover and cook for 5 to 7 minutes.

Remove the lid, stir the bok choy and add ½ teaspoon salt. Taste for flavor. If you prefer more salt, sprinkle more to desired flavor. Add the cooked shrimp and sliced green onions. Stir and cook for 1 minute, then remove from the heat.

Serve with cooked basmati rice, roti, or naan bread.

Chicken or beef can be substituted for shrimp. To prepare as a vegetarian dish, omit the meat.

renate's spin

ROASTED VEGETABLE WRAPS
SERVES 4 TO 6

What's for dinner? When faced with that question, this simple, healthy, and easy dish is the quick answer.

1   small red bell pepper, medium diced
1   small yellow bell pepper, medium diced
16 ounces portobello mushrooms, sliced
½   of a zucchini or yellow squash,
    sliced and quartered
1   small sweet Vidalia onion, diced large
4   cloves garlic, left in skins.
2-3 tablespoons extra virgin
    olive oil, divided

1   teaspoon salt
Two turns of fresh-ground black pepper
2   tablespoons pine nuts, toasted (optional)
¼   cup black olives, sliced
4   large tortilla wraps, plain or spinach flavor
Marinara sauce, store bought
10 fresh basil leaves
Shredded mozzarella cheese, (optional)

Preheat the oven to 400 F.

Place the peppers, mushrooms, zucchini or yellow squash, onion, and garlic in a roasting pan. Drizzle with 1 tablespoon olive oil, sprinkle with salt and pepper, and toss well until everything is coated.

Roast in the oven for ½ hour or until vegetables are tender and no liquid is left. Stir a few times during roasting.

When done, remove the garlic, push out the roasted cloves from the skin, and mash with a fork. Then stir the mashed garlic into the roasted vegetables.

Scrape it all into a large bowl and add the toasted pine nuts and black olives and mix well.

On a medium heated grill pan, warm a plain wrap just to make it pliable. Then spread with 1 to 2 tablespoons of marinara sauce. Top with some of the roasted vegetable mixture and fresh basil leaves. Add about ⅓ cup of shredded mozzarella cheese per wrap or more if you like.

Fold both ends over. Raise the grill temperature to hot and brush the side of the wrap that has the fold with a bit of olive oil. Place this side down on the hot grill pan and press down.

When that side has nice grill marks on it and you can hear the cheese sizzling, brush the top with olive oil and flip over. When that side is grilled nicely, remove from the pan and continue the process with the other wraps.

Slice each wrap in half at an angle and serve with green leaf salad tossed with a simple lemon, olive oil, and vinegar dressing (see page 44).

RENATE'S MEAT LOAF
SERVES 6

2 pounds lean ground beef or turkey

2 slices of white bread

½ sweet Vidalia onion, finely chopped

1 clove garlic, minced

1 carrot, peeled and finely grated

¾ cup ketchup, divided

¾ cup barbecue sauce, divided

2 tablespoons sweet chili sauce, divided

1 teaspoon kosher salt

⅓ teaspoon poultry seasoning

½ red bell pepper, finely chopped

1 tablespoon fresh parsley, finely chopped

1 large beaten egg

HERE ARE A FEW EXTRA TIPS FOR THE PERFECT MEATLOAF:

• *Before you put the meat into the loaf pan, line bottom with some bread. This will absorb all the oils and liquids.*

• *To prevent the meatloaf from cracking on top, fill a baking pan with water and place it in the oven with the meatloaf.*

Preheat oven to 375 F. Place ground meat in a large bowl.

Trim bread crusts. Chop bread into cubes, then process in a food processor to make fresh crumbs. Add breadcrumbs to the ground meat.

Add the onion, garlic, and carrot.

Mix 1 tablespoon each of the ketchup, barbecue sauce, and sweet chili sauce in a small dish and set aside. Add the rest to the meat.

Add salt, poultry seasoning, chopped red peppers, parsley, and beaten egg to the meat.

Mix well.

Place the meat mixture into a loaf pan.

Brush the ketchup, barbecue, and sweet chili sauce mixture over the top of the meat loaf.

Bake for 1 hour.

SHEILA'S LASAGNA
SERVES 8

I named this dish after my mother, Sheila, because it is her favorite. It's what she requests for Mother's Day and her birthday, and I like to think that she has all the layers of my lasagna. The sweetness of basil, the firm yet tender feel of the pasta, and the illuminating, precise ingredients in this recipe remind me of all the dimensions my mother reaches. She will always greet you with a smile and treat you with as much care and attention as the detailed steps of preparing the ribbons of this dish. She is as sharp, bright, and spicy as the pleasant heat of red pepper flakes, and at the end of the day, she is warm and gentle with open arms you can melt into. We all have traits under the surface, each unique and incomparable, just like lasagna!

1	tablespoon olive oil
¼	cup sweet Vidalia onion, medium diced
2	cloves garlic, finely chopped
1	red bell pepper, medium diced
1	yellow bell pepper, medium diced
8	ounces portabello mushrooms, sliced
16	ounces spinach leaves, thoroughly rinsed
1	pound ground turkey
1	teaspoon adobo all-purpose seasoning
1	medium carrot, peeled and finely grated
4	cups tomato pasta sauce

½	teaspoon oregano
1	teaspoon crushed red pepper flakes
10	fresh basil leaves, coarsely chopped
1	tablespoon salt
1	tablespoon canola or vegetable oil
9	lasagna noodles
	Cooking spray
4	cups shredded mozzarella cheese
1	cup grated Italian cheese blend (Parmesan, Asiago, and Romano)
	Salt to taste

QUICK TIP

This dish pairs well with a garden salad, garlic bread, and bruschetta. It's an easy menu and perfect for entertaining guests. It can also be made meatless by substituting the meat with your favorite cooked vegetables. Also feel free to play around with cheeses of your choice. That is what I did and came up with my own style of lasagna. I do not like ricotta cheese; hence, no ricotta is included in this recipe.

In a large skillet, heat the olive oil on medium and then add the chopped onions, garlic, bell peppers, and mushrooms. Cook until tender.

Add the spinach and cook until it wilts. Remove vegetables from the skillet.

Add the ground turkey, sprinkle with adobo seasoning, and stir until the meat crumbles and is no longer pink. Drain any liquid and then stir in the cooked vegetables, shredded carrot, and pasta sauce. Sprinkle with oregano and crushed red pepper flakes and let simmer to combine. Taste for desired flavor. Turn off the heat and stir in the chopped basil. Let the mixture cool.

In a large pot of water, add salt and vegetable oil and bring to a boil. Add the noodles and cook for 15 minutes for a tender consistency. Drain the noodles.

Lightly coat a 13x9-inch baking dish with cooking spray.

Layer 3 noodles, spread one-third of the meat sauce, and then layer with one-third of mozzarella cheese and Italian blend cheese. Repeat for the second layer. For the third layer, place the 3 noodles and spread the remaining meat sauce but do not add cheese at this point.

Cover the baking dish with aluminum foil and bake at 375 F for 30 minutes.

Uncover then sprinkle the remaining mozzarella and Italian blend cheese and bake for 5 more minutes or until the cheese is melted and bubbly.

Let stand 15 minutes before serving.

KEITH'S GRILLED SALMON

SERVES 6-8

My husband has given me so much: my home, my children, and a great life. Yet there is one thing that tops them all: his gift of grilled salmon. OK, maybe that's an exaggeration, but this dish came into my life at a time when I felt completely overwhelmed with the daily tasks of work and family. My loving husband, Keith, quickly saw I was at the end of my rope and stepped in to help out with dinner. Keith is not exactly known for his cooking, but when he does step up to the "plate," he impresses even the harshest critic. This dish reminds me of what it feels like to be supported. I'm also reminded that when we allow ourselves to release expectations, we may be pleasantly surprised.

2   pounds salmon fillet (about 5 pieces)
2   teaspoons smoked sweet paprika
2   teaspoons adobo seasoning
2   teaspoons creole seasoning
¼   cup red bell peppers, finely chopped
¼   cup yellow bell peppers, finely chopped

1   scallion, thinly sliced
2   cloves garlic, minced
1   teaspoon fresh thyme, minced
2   tablespoons olive oil
Fresh-ground black pepper

QUICK TIP

Thyme is stunning with this salmon. Take the advice of "thyme" and take time for yourself and remember those who support you!

Preheat the outdoor grill.

Place the fillets on a large sheet of nonstick aluminum foil.

In a small bowl, mix together all of the ingredients except the olive oil and black pepper. Rub the mixture on top of the fillets, coating very well.

Sprinkle with fresh-ground black pepper, then drizzle with olive oil. Fold the foil to wrap the fish.

Grill for 10 to 15 minutes or until the fish flakes easily with a fork. Serve warm.

Alternatively, the fish can be roasted in a 400 F oven for 10 to 15 minutes.

For a complete meal, serve with roasted sweet potatoes (page 38).

ROASTED SWEET POTATOES
SERVES 6

3   whole sweet potatoes, peeled and cut into bite-size cubes

1   tablespoon brown sugar

1   teaspoon ground cinnamon

¼   teaspoon ground nutmeg

⅓   teaspoon ground ginger

Sea salt to taste

1   tablespoon butter

2   teaspoons olive oil

1   tablespoon fresh parsley for garnish, finely chopped

Preheat the oven to 350 F.

Line a baking dish with foil or coat with cooking spray.

Place cubed potatoes in a bowl and add brown sugar, cinnamon, nutmeg, ginger, and salt. Mix well.

Melt butter in the microwave and pour over the potatoes along with the olive oil. Add more sugar or cinnamon if desired.

Toss to coat evenly.

Pour the potatoes into the baking dish and roast for 1 hour. Stir the sweet potatoes once or twice during roasting.

When finished, garnish with chopped parsley.

RIB EYE STEAKS
SERVES 4 TO 6

4   rib eye steaks
¼   cup low sodium soy sauce
½   cup olive oil
¼   cup Worcestershire sauce
¼   cup steak sauce
4   cloves garlic, peeled and minced
1   teaspoon fresh-grated ginger
4   tablespoons brown sugar
1   teaspoon adobo all-purpose seasoning
1   teaspoon red pepper flakes

Lay the steaks flat in a casserole dish.

In a large bowl, combine all remaining ingredients. Mix well. Pour over the steaks and turn once to incorporate marinade. Cover with plastic wrap and refrigerate overnight.

One hour before grilling, remove the steaks from the refrigerator and let them come to room temperature.

Remove the steaks from the marinade and pat with a paper towel.

Grill on medium heat for 10 to 15 minutes, turning a few times, and cook to desired doneness.

Meanwhile, prepare the rosemary potatoes (right).

ROSEMARY POTATOES
SERVES 6

10 red or golden potatoes
½   cup olive oil
4   teaspoons fresh rosemary, finely chopped
3   cloves fresh garlic, minced
1   tablespoon kosher salt
2   turns of fresh-ground black pepper
½   tablespoon paprika
1   tablespoon fresh parsley, finely chopped (set aside)

Heat the oven to 400 F.

Line a large casserole dish with foil.

Wash and dry the potatoes. Leaving the skin on, dice the potatoes into small cubes.

In a large bowl, combine the potatoes, olive oil, rosemary, garlic, salt, pepper, and paprika. Mix well.

Place the potatoes into the casserole dish and cook for 35 to 45 minutes.

After 30 minutes, test for tenderness and flavor. Add more salt and pepper if desired.

When the potatoes are finished, remove them from the oven, sprinkle the chopped parsley on top, and stir.

Serve warm with the rib eye steaks.

REN'S MACARONI CASSEROLE
SERVES 8 TO 10

This easy recipe is sure to change the way you cook your next batch of mac & cheese. You will experience the flavor of fresh ingredients with every bite.

1   pound (16 ounces) elbow macaroni, uncooked

1   quart (4 cups) 2% milk

1   stick unsalted butter

½   cup all-purpose flour

12   ounces (4 cups) grated Gruyère, Fontina or shredded mozzarella cheese

8   ounces (2 cups) grated sharp cheddar cheese

¼   cup grated Parmesan cheese for sprinkling

Salt

Cooking spray

Preheat oven to 375 F.

Cook the macaroni according to package directions. Drain and set aside.

Heat the milk in a small saucepan. Don't boil.

Melt the butter in a large pot on low heat. Sprinkle in the flour and whisk over low heat for 2 minutes.

Continue whisking and add the hot milk. Cook for another two minutes until thick and smooth. Remove from heat and add the Gruyère, Fontina, or mozzarella cheese and the cheddar cheese and salt to taste.

Add cooked macaroni and stir well.

Spray a large casserole dish with cooking spray. Pour the macaroni into the dish and sprinkle the top with grated Parmesan cheese.

Bake for 35 minutes or until bubbly and lightly golden brown.

SUMMER CHICKEN SALAD
SERVES 4

I love the combination of chicken, melon, grapes, nuts, cheese, and mixed salad greens in this refreshing salad. Feel free to use your favorite summer fruits and nuts in place of these suggestions if you wish.

2 cups sliced, cooked chicken breast

½ cup plain Greek yogurt

1 to 2 tablespoons apple cider or white wine vinegar (or to taste)

1½ teaspoons sunflower seeds or poppy seeds

¼ teaspoon salt

Fresh-ground black pepper to taste

2 bags of mixed salad greens

2 cups diced melon, such as cantaloupe or honeydew

1 cup red seedless grapes

¼ cup sunflower seeds or chopped walnuts

¼ cup crumbled feta or goat cheese

QUICK TIP

To poach chicken breasts for this recipe, place ¾ pounds of boneless, skinless chicken breasts in a medium skillet or saucepan and cover with low-sodium chicken broth. Bring to a boil. Cover, reduce heat to low, and simmer gently until the chicken is cooked through and no longer pink in the middle, 10 to 12 minutes. Remove the chicken from the broth and let it cool before cutting into small or medium pieces.

Whisk yogurt, vinegar, sunflower or poppy seeds, salt, and pepper in a large bowl until smooth. Reserve ¼ cup of the dressing in a small bowl. Add the mixed greens to the large bowl and toss to coat. Divide among plates and top with chicken, melon, grapes, nuts, and cheese. Drizzle each portion with 1 tablespoon of the reserved dressing.

SIMPLE SAMOSA SMACKERS
SERVES 6

2 medium gold potatoes, unpeeled and cut in half

14 ounces extra firm tofu, crumbled, nonfrozen

1 medium sweet yellow onion, finely chopped

1 cup frozen green peas

1 medium tomato, diced

1 tablespoon fresh ginger, peeled and minced

½ jalapeno pepper, stemmed, seeded, and finely diced

1 tablespoon olive oil

2 tablespoons plus ½ cup water

Salt to taste

2 teaspoons curry powder

¼ teaspoon garam masala

½ teaspoon ground coriander

¾ teaspoon ground cumin

⅓ teaspoon cayenne pepper (or to taste)

1 tablespoon fresh lemon juice

6 whole grain or plain flour tortillas or mini pitas

In a medium pot of lightly salted water, add potatoes and cook until tender (pierce easily with a fork). Drain and set aside to cool. When cool enough to handle, peel and cut into ¼-inch cubes.

Squeeze the tofu to remove as much water as possible. Cut into ¼-inch cubes.

Heat the olive oil in a deep nonstick skillet, then add the onion. Cook on medium-high until the onion begins to brown. Add peas, tomato, ginger, jalapeno pepper, and 2 tablespoons of water. Cook, stirring, until the peas thaw.

Add potatoes and tofu to the skillet along with ½ cup water, salt, curry powder, garam masala, coriander, cumin, cayenne, and lemon juice. Cover and simmer for about 10 minutes, adding more water if necessary. Remove cover and cook until most liquid has evaporated. Taste for flavor. Add more salt or lemon juice if needed.

Warm the tortillas according to the package directions. Place 3 tablespoons of filling in the center of each wrap, fold bottom edge up, and fold sides over filling. (If using mini pitas, make an opening down the middle and stuff with filling.)

Serve with fresh or jarred mango chutney or salsa if desired.

Another delightful way to enjoy these Samosas is to turn them into light and crispy appetizers (as pictured) by using packaged wonton or spring roll wraps. Shape into triangles and bake at 350 F for 10-12 minutes.

Here's what you will need: 1 package wonton or spring roll wraps (can be found in frozen section of grocery store) and cooking spray or olive oil (for brushing tops of samosas).

Method: Scoop 1 tablespoon of the filling onto wonton wrapper; brush the two sides with water and fold to form a triangle. Press the edge to make a seal. Set aside on a baking sheet lined with parchment paper. Repeat until all ingredients are used.

Spray samosas with cooking spray or brush lightly with olive oil and bake in pre-heated 350 F oven for 10-12 minutes or until golden brown.

Enjoy with your favorite dipping sauce.

SCRUMPTIOUS CHICKEN PARM
& LEMON VINAIGRETTE MIXED GREENS
SERVES 6

Testing this recipe was another of my tricky ways of getting my son, Keith Jr., to eat salad. He loves this chicken but dislikes salad. I turned the love-hate relationship into a delicious meal that he now enjoys. The trick was putting the salad on the hot chicken cutlet, then adding extra Parmesan cheese. The warmth of the chicken created a delicious flavor and texture to the salad. This made him feel like he was eating spinach. He loves spinach!

For the Chicken Parm:

4 to 6 boneless, skinless chicken breasts

1   cup all-purpose flour

1   teaspoon kosher salt

½   teaspoon fresh-ground black pepper

2   extra-large eggs

1   tablespoon water

1¼ cups seasoned dry bread crumbs

½   cup fresh grated Parmesan
    cheese, plus extra for serving

Unsalted butter, for frying

Olive oil

For the Salad:

6   cups mixed greens, washed and spun dry

¼   cup sliced almonds or
    sunflower seeds (optional)

For the Lemon Vinaigrette:

¼   cup fresh squeezed lemon
    juice (2 large lemons)

½   cup good olive oil

½   teaspoon kosher salt

¼   teaspoon fresh-ground black pepper

Place the chicken breasts in plastic wrap and pound until they are ¼-inch thick. You can use either a meat mallet or a rolling pin.

On a large plate, combine the flour, salt, and pepper.

On a second plate, beat the eggs with 1 tablespoon of water.

On a third plate, combine the bread crumbs and ½ cup grated Parmesan.

Coat the chicken breasts on both sides with the flour mixture, then dip both sides into the egg mixture, and dredge both sides in the bread-crumb mixture, pressing lightly.

Heat 1 tablespoon of butter and 1 tablespoon of olive oil in a large sauté pan and cook 2 or 3 chicken breasts on medium-low heat for 2 to 3 minutes on each side, until cooked through.

Continue the process, adding more butter and oil and cook the rest of the chicken breasts.

Now prepare the salad and vinaigrette. In a small bowl, whisk together the lemon juice, olive oil, salt, and pepper.

In a large bowl, toss the salad greens with the lemon vinaigrette. Sprinkle with sliced almonds or sunflower seeds.

To each serving plate, place a piece of hot chicken breast and a mound of salad on top of the chicken.

Serve with extra grated Parmesan.

CHA-CHA CHILI

SERVES 10

For quite some time, I would suffer indigestion after consuming certain meals. I later discovered an allergy to beef. At first, I was stuck in a holding pattern of turmoiled thoughts that I would have to live without juicy steak or ground beef, meaning no more chili! I refused to take that as an option and began exploring other ways to satisfy my craving for this adored comfort food.

I studied the ingredients of all my favorite chilis and made the bold choice of substituting ground beef with chicken. I've found that the spice variety in this recipe surprisingly makes an even deeper impression on the chicken than the beef. Cha-Cha Chili is the perfect alternative to the same old chili recipe and a perfect way to change things up.

10 plum tomatoes, halved lengthwise	1 tablespoon adobo all-purpose seasoning
1 jalapeno pepper, halved and seeded (optional)	½ teaspoon poultry seasoning
1 sweet white onion, peeled and halved	⅓ teaspoon sweet paprika
4 garlic cloves, peeled	1 teaspoon Worcestershire sauce
2 tablespoons olive oil	1 chipotle chili pepper in adobo sauce, seeded and finely chopped (get the smallest can and refrigerate the rest for future use)
4 to 6 skinless, boneless chicken thighs cut into very small cubes	
¼ cup chili powder	1¾ cups chicken or vegetable broth
1 tablespoon creole seasoning (such as Tony Chachere)	1 can (15 ounces) cannellini or dark red kidney beans, rinsed and drained
2 teaspoons salt	2 tablespoons fresh chopped parsley

QUICK TIP

Try this recipe with these great pairings: sweet corn bread (see Grandma's Famous Corn Muffins recipe on page 56), fragrant jasmine rice, and a mixed greens salad.

Place the chicken in a casserole dish and season with creole seasoning, adobo seasoning, poultry seasoning, paprika, and Worcestershire sauce. Marinate for 30 minutes.

Preheat oven broiler with rack about 3 inches from heat source.

Arrange tomatoes, jalapeno, onion and garlic, cut side down on a foil lined baking sheet. Broil until starting to char, about 10-15 minutes. Remove from oven, let cool then pulse tomatoes and jalapeno in a blender or food processor until chunky or smooth (as desired).

Separately, chop onions and mince the garlic.

Heat a large pot over medium-high heat; add olive oil; add the chicken and cook until brown for 5-10 minutes. Remove and set aside.

In the same pot, add onions and garlic and cook until soft and golden, about 5 minutes.

Add chili powder and 2 teaspoons salt. Cook, stirring for one minute; stir in chipotle pepper and add chicken, raise heat to high. Stir in tomato mixture; cook for 3- 5 minutes, scraping up browned bits.

Stir in broth; simmer for 20 minutes. Taste for desired flavor. Add beans and simmer for 10 minutes, turn off the heat and stir in the parsley leaves.

Serve and enjoy warm.

LEMON PARSLEY LINGUINI

SERVES 6

1 tablespoon plus 1 teaspoon salt, divided

1 tablespoon canola or vegetable oil

16 ounces (1 box) linguini pasta

½ cup olive oil

5 cloves garlic, minced

½ cup low-sodium chicken
or vegetable broth

½ teaspoon fresh-ground black pepper

1 medium lemon, zested and juiced

¾ cup grated Parmesan cheese

½ cup parsley, finely chopped

Add 1 tablespoon salt to a large pot of water and bring to a boil. Add canola oil and linguini. Stirring frequently, cook until the linguine is tender but firm, about 8 to10 minutes, then drain in a colander.

To the same pasta pot, heat the olive oil on low heat, then add the minced garlic, stirring until soft and fragrant, about 2 minutes. Be sure not to burn the garlic.

Add the pasta back to the pot, then add the chicken broth, 1 teaspoon salt, and pepper. Toss to combine and cook for 2 minutes

Add ½ teaspoon of the lemon juice, lemon zest, and grated Parmesan cheese and toss to combine. Taste for desired flavor. Add more salt, pepper, or lemon juice if needed. Sprinkle with the fresh chopped parsley.

Stir, serve, and enjoy.

PENNE & SUN-DRIED TOMATOES

SERVES 8

¼ cup olive oil

5 garlic cloves, peeled and sliced in half

12 ounces penne pasta, uncooked

½ cup chopped sun-dried tomatoes and capers packed in olive oil

½ cup red bell peppers, diced small

1 teaspoon garlic powder

¼ cup freshly grated Parmesan cheese

Salt and pepper to taste

QUICK TIP

This pasta dish is so easy to make yet very delicious. It is perfect for a quick, healthy dinner and quite filling. It beautifully complements baked chicken and grilled fish.

In a small pan, add the olive oil and garlic and roast over medium heat, keeping a close eye so as not to burn the garlic.

In a large pot, cook the pasta according to package directions. Drain and return the pasta to the pot.

Add the roasted garlic and olive oil, chopped sun-dried tomatoes and capers, and bell peppers. Mix to combine.

Stir in the garlic powder and freshly grated Parmesan cheese.

Season the pasta to taste with salt and pepper. Add more cheese and olive oil if needed.

Serve warm.

CHICKEN MARSALA MADE EASY
SERVES 4

The name alone, "chicken marsala," made me think this was a complex dish to make when I first tasted it in a restaurant. I decided to research how it was made, and indeed it sounded like a lot of work. But I was determined to make it, and with a few tweaks, I put my spin on it and came up with an easier method without compromising the deliciousness. To put this into recipe form, I had to tumble through my "toss box" to find my sticky note where I jotted down how I made it. Actually, this can be said for almost all of my recipes since I learned to cook by tossing, dashing, and averaging ingredients, hence another reason why it took me a while to finish this cookbook.

4 skinless, boneless, chicken breasts
All-purpose flour for dredging
Kosher salt and ground black pepper
½ teaspoon lemon garlic spice blend
½ teaspoon sweet paprika
¼ cup olive oil (maybe more if needed)

2 cloves garlic, minced
8 ounces sliced cremini mushrooms
3 sage leaves, chopped small
½ cup marsala wine
2 tablespoons butter
¼ cup chopped flat-leaf parsley

Place the chicken breasts side by side on a cutting board and lay a piece of plastic wrap over them; pound with a flat meat mallet or rolling pin until they are tenderized, about ¼-inch thick.

Add some flour to a shallow plate and season with a fair amount of salt and pepper, lemon garlic blend spice, and sweet paprika; mix with a fork to distribute evenly. Set aside.

Heat the oil over medium-high heat in a large skillet. Add the minced garlic, sliced mushrooms and chopped sage and cook until nicely browned. Remove and set aside.

Add some more oil to the skillet. When the oil is nice and hot, dredge both sides of the chicken cutlets in the seasoned flour, shaking off the excess. Place the cutlets into the pan and fry for 5 minutes on each side until golden, turning once. Do this in batches if the pieces don't fit comfortably in the pan. Remove the chicken to a large platter in a single layer to keep warm.

Add the marsala and butter to the pan and boil down for a few seconds to cook out the alcohol and simmer for 1 minute to thicken the sauce slightly. Add the chicken and mushrooms to the pan; simmer gently for 1 minute to heat the chicken through. Season with salt and pepper and garnish with chopped parsley before serving.

This dish pairs well with oven-roasted potatoes.

breakfast delights

FENTON'S FAMOUS FRITATTA

SERVES 6 TO 8

This frittata became famous in our household when my brother, Fenton, volunteered to make breakfast one morning while visiting for the holidays. It became a hit since then and has become our New Years' morning breakfast replacing the old tradition of pepperpot (a recipe for another time) and bread. Every time he visits now, we ask him, "When are you making frittata?" And when he does, we are punctual at the breakfast table waiting to devour.

You will need an oven-proof pan or skillet for this recipe. Stainless steel, nonstick, or cast iron work, as long as it is oven proof (no wood, rubber, or plastic handles).

6 to 8 eggs, room temperature

1 teaspoon Tony Chachere's creole seasoning

Pinch of salt

1 tablespoon olive oil or butter

½ cup chopped spinach

½ cup mushrooms, sliced

¼ cup green bell pepper, medium chopped

¼ cup red bell pepper, medium chopped

½ cup zucchini, chopped small

Half of a sweet onion, medium chopped

½ to 1 cup shredded Parmesan cheese

1 green onion, chopped small

Fresh-ground black pepper

Tomatoes for garnish (optional)

QUICK TIP

You can use other cheeses in this recipe, but I think Parmesan makes a nice flavor.

Preheat the oven broiler to low.

In a medium bowl, beat the eggs and add some ground pepper, the creole seasoning, and salt. You could add some Parmesan cheese at this point if desired but not too much.

In your oven-proof pan, heat the olive oil or butter and sauté the vegetables. Considering reserving 1 teaspoon green onions to sprinkle on top of the frittata before placing it in the oven. Don't overcook the vegetables. Spread the vegetables evenly in the pan then pour beaten eggs over the vegetables. Don't stir or mix. Just pour the eggs over the veggies.

Cook over low heat for about 8 to 10 minutes until the eggs are starting to set. DON'T stir.

Sprinkle Parmesan cheese on top of the eggs. Be generous. You could also sprinkle some chopped green onion on top if you want.

Place the pan in the oven on the middle shelf, which will help prevent burning. Cook until the top (cheese and egg) is cooked and starts to turn brown, about 5 to 6 minutes. Don't overcook. However, make sure the top of the eggs are cooked and not watery.

Remove from the oven and let cool.

Use a spatula to carefully loosen the edges all around before transferring to a serving platter. Place the platter on top of the pan and flip the pan over, so the frittata is now on the platter (just as you would if trying to remove a cake out of a pan). The vegetables should be facing up.

Cut and serve.

If desired, garnish with slices of fresh tomatoes on top or on the side.

ORANGE PECAN MAPLE FRENCH TOAST
SERVES 6

7 large eggs

1½ cups milk (whole or 2%)

1½ cups plus 2 tablespoons maple syrup

2 teaspoons ground cinnamon

1 teaspoon ground nutmeg

½ teaspoon ground cardamom

Zest of one orange

3 teaspoons almond extract

3 teaspoons vanilla extract

12 slices brioche bread

1 cup pecans, toasted and chopped

4 ounces (1 stick) butter

Confectioners' sugar and orange
    slices for serving

In a large bowl, whisk together the eggs and milk.

Add the 2 tablespoons maple syrup, cinnamon, nutmeg, cardamom, and orange zest to the egg and milk mixture. Stir in the almond and vanilla extracts and whisk well.

Working with one slice of bread at a time, put a slice into the egg mixture and let it soak for about 15 seconds on each side. Place on a rimmed baking sheet to rest while all the bread is dipped and the griddle pan is heated.

In a medium nonstick skillet or griddle pan set over medium heat, melt 2 tablespoons of butter.

Place 2 or 3 slices of bread into the pan and cook for about 2 minutes per side until golden brown on each side. Add a bit more butter to the pan after you flip the bread, if needed.

Transfer to a heatproof plate and set aside. Cover with a kitchen towel and keep warm in the oven while you cook the remainder of the toast. Repeat the cooking process with remaining bread.

Meanwhile, toast the pecans. Heat oven to 350 F. Place pecans in a baking sheet and toast for 8 minutes or until golden brown. Remove from the oven and chop into medium pieces. Set aside.

Warm the maple syrup in a microwave-safe cup.

To serve, place 2 slices of French toast on each plate. Drizzle with warm maple syrup and generously sprinkle with toasted pecans and dust with confectioners' sugar.

Garnish with orange slices and serve immediately.

EGGCELLENT SUNDAY BREAKFAST

SERVES 4

Growing up, this was a classic Sunday breakfast that my mom prepared for our family. We enjoyed it with cups of hot tea. I still recollect the tea leaves steeping in her beautiful teapot, which I inherited. The best part for me was the orange marmalade Dad would spread on top of the melted butter on warm toast. I liked the edges of my eggs crispy, so my mom would cook my egg a little longer, and that is how this over-easy egg gained its crispy edges. This simple recipe is an "eggcellent" way to bring the family together for Sunday breakfast.

4 large brown eggs

4 tablespoons butter

Black pepper and salt (optional)

8 slices bread, honey wheat, whole grain or bread of your choice

Butter and orange marmalade, for spreading (recommend Duerr's English Traditional Fine Cut Marmalade)

Heat a small nonstick frying pan on low heat.

Add 1 tablespoon butter and melt. Crack one egg and gently place in pan. Sprinkle with black pepper and salt (if desired). Cook for 1 minute until the edges of the egg becomes light brown and crisp. Using a spatula, gently flip the egg over and cook for ½ minute. Remove and place on a plate.

Repeat the process with remaining eggs.

Serve each egg with toasted bread slices spread with butter and orange marmalade. The warmth of the toast will nicely melt the butter and warm the marmalade, producing a satisfying crunch with every bite along with the glorious egg.

Enjoy with cups of hot tea.

SCONES & TEA
MAKES: 10

"Scones and tea for my daughter and me." This was a little tune I made up when my daughter, Kellie, was a little girl and we had our weekend tea party. She set the table with her china doll tea ware and then helped me make scones and steep teas for our mother-daughter day. Now Kellie is all grown up and isn't too into my made up melodies, but every so often, she spares a moment to have scones and tea with me sans my musical interludes.

2   cups all-purpose flour

½   cup granulated sugar

2   teaspoons baking powder

¼   cup (4 tablespoons) cold butter, cubed

1   cup raisins or currants

½   cup milk, plus more for glazing, room temperature

1   egg, room temperature

Orange marmalade

Clotted cream

QUICK TIP

Dried cranberries with grated orange zest can be substituted for raisins and currants.

Preheat oven to 400 F. Line a baking sheet with parchment paper.

In a large bowl, combine the flour, sugar, and baking powder. Cut in the butter until the mixture resembles fine crumbs.

Stir in the raisins or currants.

Beat ½ cup milk and egg, then add to the dry ingredient mixture. Stir lightly to combine.

On a lightly floured board, roll dough to 1-inch thickness. Cut into circles with a 2½-inch biscuit cutter. Brush tops with milk.

Bake for 10 to 15 minutes or until golden brown.

Serve warm with orange marmalade and clotted cream.

APPLE BANANA MUFFINS

MAKES: 10

¼ cup (4 tablespoons) butter, melted

¼ cup plus 2 teaspoons coconut palm sugar (or light brown sugar)

1 large egg

1 teaspoon vanilla

1 banana, peeled and mashed with a fork

½ of an apple, finely chopped

1 cup plus 2 tablespoons all-purpose flour

1 teaspoon baking powder

¼ teaspoon baking soda

½ teaspoon ground cinnamon

½ teaspoon kosher salt

1 tablespoon flaxseed meal

QUICK TIP

Blueberries, strawberries, or pineapple can be used in place of apples.

Preheat oven to 350 F.

Line a muffin pan with paper cups or spray with nonstick baking spray.

Melt butter and set aside.

In a medium bowl, mix the coconut palm sugar, egg, vanilla, banana, and apples. Add melted butter and stir.

Add dry ingredients to wet ingredients and stir only to combine. Do not over mix. Fill muffin cups ⅔ full with the batter.

Bake until center comes clean when a tester is inserted, about 20 to 25 minutes.

Remove from oven and cool on baking rack.

GRANDMA'S LOVIN' CORN MUFFINS

MAKES: 24

These muffins earned their title when my mom made them for my children when they were little. They noticed the difference in flavor and texture compared to an instant muffin mix. After eating these corn muffins, they would insist that I make "Grandma's muffins." So I had to acquire the method from my mom and turned them into a recipe because she doesn't measure; she averages and relates to measuring as "a heaping pot spoon of this" or "an eating spoon of that." These little treats are easy to make, and it's such a difference to eat food that has been infused with a personal touch of love.

1 stick (4 ounces) unsalted butter, melted

½ cup canola oil

½ cup granulated sugar

4 eggs, room temperature

1 cup milk, room temperature

2 cups corn meal

2 cups all-purpose flour

4 teaspoons baking powder

continued on following page

continued from previous page

Preheat the oven to 350 F. Line two 12-cup muffin pans with cupcake liners.

In a large bowl, combine butter, oil, and sugar and mix well. Whisk in eggs and milk.

Fold in the dry ingredients.

Divide the batter among the lined muffin pans and bake for 20 to 25 minutes to a golden color and when a tester inserted in the center of muffins comes out clean.

ZUCCHINI WALNUT MUFFINS
MAKES: 12

- 1⅓ cups all-purpose flour
- ½ cup brown sugar or coconut palm sugar
- 1 teaspoon baking powder
- 2 tablespoons ground flaxseed meal
- 1 teaspoon ground cinnamon
- ½ teaspoon ground cardamom
- ¼ teaspoon ground allspice
- ½ teaspoon kosher salt
- ⅔ cup shredded zucchini (about 1 medium zucchini)
- 3 tablespoons canola oil
- 2 tablespoons butter, melted
- 2 tablespoons milk
- 1 teaspoon vanilla extract
- 1 large egg, beaten
- 12 walnut pieces

Preheat oven to 400 F. Line a 12-cup muffin tin with cupcake liners or spray with cooking spray.

In a large mixing bowl, add flour, brown sugar, baking powder, ground flax meal, cinnamon, cardamom, allspice, and salt and stir to combine.

In another bowl, combine zucchini, oil, melted butter, milk, vanilla, and egg. Whisk well. Add the zucchini mixture to the flour mixture and stir until the batter combines.

Using an ice cream scoop or spoon, scoop batter and fill the muffin cups ⅔ full.

Top each muffin with one walnut piece.

Bake for 15 to 18 minutes or until a tester inserted in the center of muffins comes out clean.

CHAI BREAKFAST BUNS
MAKES: 24 TO 27

6 tablespoons tepid (warm tap) water	¼ teaspoon nutmeg
5 teaspoons yeast	¼ teaspoon cardamom
2½ cups milk	3 tablespoons almond extract
1 chai tea sachet	2 teaspoons vanilla extract
1 stick (4 ounces) unsalted butter, melted	1 cup raisins
1 cup granulated sugar	7 cups flour, more for kneading
2 eggs, room temperature and beaten	Maple syrup, for glaze
2 tablespoons ground flaxseed meal	
¼ teaspoon cinnamon	

QUICK TIP

These buns are delicious when sliced and buttered along with a piece of cheddar cheese. It's a healthy way to start the day. Dried cranberries are a great substitute for raisins.

In a small bowl add, combine the water and yeast. Let set for about 8 to 10 minutes.

In a medium saucepan, heat milk over low heat. Add the chai tea sachet and let steep while the milk warms.

Add melted butter and sugar and stir to dissolve. Do not boil the milk. Remove and discard the tea sachet.

In a large bowl, pour the milk mixture, add the yeast and two beaten eggs. Whisk well to combine.

Add ground flaxseed meal, cinnamon, nutmeg and cardamom and whisk well.

Add almond and vanilla extracts and raisins.

Add flour one cup at a time and mix to form a soft dough.

Let dough rest for 5 minutes.

Turn onto a floured surface and knead until smooth and elastic, about 8 to 10 minutes. Place in a greased bowl, turning once to grease top. Cover and let rise in a warm place until doubled in size, about 1 hour.

Punch dough down and divide in half. Knead each half then shape into 2-inch balls. Place 2 inches apart on baking sheets lined with parchment paper or greased with cooking spray.

Cover and let rise until doubled, about 10 minutes.

Preheat oven to 325 F.

Mist or brush tops of the buns with water then bake for 25 to 30 minutes or until golden brown. Cool on wire racks. Glaze each bun with maple syrup.

AUTHENTIC BANANA BREAD

MAKES 6-8 SERVINGS

This recipe is easy to make and delicious to the last crumb! I've tasted quite a lot of banana bread, but there is nothing compared to this. Even if you're not fond of coconut, you will enjoy it in this bread. A conversation between my brother and me about banana bread turned into my spin on a basic recipe, and I came up with this easy and uncomplicated method that produces heavenly slices of bread.

1½ to 2 cups mashed bananas
  (4 to 5 yellow bananas)
¾ cup vegetable oil
2 eggs at room temperature
¾ cup granulated sugar
2 cups all-purpose flour

½ cup chopped walnuts
¾ cup sweetened coconut flakes
1 teaspoon baking soda
½ teaspoon baking powder
½ teaspoon salt
1 teaspoon almond extract

Preheat oven to 325 F.
  Grease a 5x9-inch loaf pan.
  In a large bowl, use a wooden spoon to combine the bananas, oil, and eggs.
  Fold in remaining ingredients and mix well.
  Pour the batter into the loaf pan and bake on the oven's top rack.
  Bake 60 to 70 minutes or until a toothpick comes out clean.
  Cool 10 minutes in the pan.
  Remove and cool completely before slicing.

soups

EXOTIC VEGETABLE & CHICKEN DUMPLING SOUP

SERVES ABOUT 10

For the Chicken:

2   pounds chicken, cut into 1-inch pieces

1   teaspoon adobo seasoning

1   teaspoon paprika

½   teaspoon salt

Fresh-ground black pepper

1   tablespoon cassareep or browning sauce (found in international aisle)

For the Dumplings:

¾   cup all-purpose flour

½   teaspoon baking powder

½   teaspoon salt

½   teaspoon pure cane sugar

1   tablespoon butter

¼   cup water

For the Soup:

2   medium cassavas (yucca), peeled and chopped into 2-inch pieces

5   eddos (taro), peeled and chopped into 2-inch pieces

2   green plantains, sliced into 1½-inch pieces

2   sweet potatoes, peeled and chopped into 2-inch pieces

1   tablespoon olive or canola oil

1   sweet onion, chopped

¼   cup red bell peppers, chopped

¼   cup yellow bell peppers, chopped

2   celery stalks, chopped

3   garlic cloves, minced

16   cups chicken or vegetable broth

½   cup barley, rinsed and soaked for 10 minutes

2   large chicken bouillon cubes

2   bay leaves

Salt and pepper to taste

Water or more broth, if needed

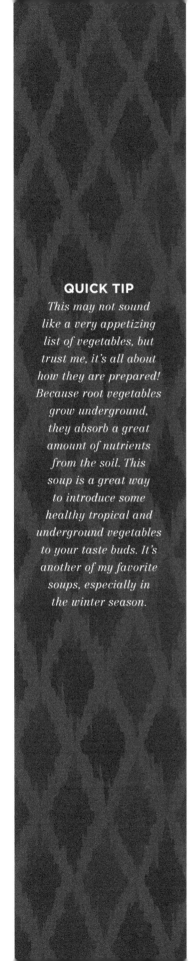

QUICK TIP

This may not sound like a very appetizing list of vegetables, but trust me, it's all about how they are prepared! Because root vegetables grow underground, they absorb a great amount of nutrients from the soil. This soup is a great way to introduce some healthy tropical and underground vegetables to your taste buds. It's another of my favorite soups, especially in the winter season.

Season the chicken with all of the spices and browning sauce, then set aside.

Rinse the peeled and chopped yucca, eddoes, sweet potatoes, and plantains and soak in cold water.

In a large stock pot, heat the oil and cook the chopped onions, peppers, celery, and minced garlic. Cook for 3 to 4 minutes, stirring frequently.

Add the chicken, stir, cover, and cook for about 8 to 10 minutes until browned and fully cooked.

Pour in the broth and add the barley, bouillon, and bay leaves.

Cover the pot and boil for 10 minutes.

Drain the root vegetables and add to the pot.

Add salt and pepper. Give it a good stir. If you feel this needs more liquid, you can add more broth or water at this point.

Cover, reduce heat to medium, and let the flavors simmer together and vegetables cook until they are medium-soft, about 20 minutes.

While the vegetables are cooking, make the dough for the dumplings. (It will be a semi-stiff dough, which is OK.) Stir together flour, baking powder, salt, and sugar in a medium size bowl. Cut in butter until crumbly. Stir in the water to make a medium-textured, stiff dough (not too soft, not too stiff).

Once the root vegetables, potatoes, and plantains are cooked through, use a teaspoon to scoop small pieces of dumpling dough and drop them deep into the soup. The dumplings will cook in approximately 5 minutes. Stir the soup as you drop the dumplings in.

Once all of the dumplings are in the pot, cover and let simmer for an additional 10 minutes without removing the lid.

Remove and discard bay leaves and serve warm.

INNER PEAS SOUP
SERVES ABOUT 10

Pantry staples solved a soup-of-the-day crisis and became a favorite. Once when my youngest was not feeling well, I decided to make her some chicken barley soup only to discover when I opened the pantry that I was out of barley! But lying there was a bag of dried green split peas. I was pleasantly surprised when I had concocted this soup from almost nothing, and it turned out so delicious that my daughter enjoyed it and began to feel better, achieving her inner "peas" (peace). This is now an often-requested soup for the cold season.

1   teaspoon olive oil

1   sweet onion, medium diced

½   red bell pepper, medium diced

½   yellow bell pepper, medium diced

2   celery stalks, medium diced

2   cloves garlic, minced

1   bag (16 ounces) green split peas, rinsed well and soaked for at least 30 minutes

4   cups chicken or vegetable broth, more if needed

2   bay leaves

2   chicken or vegetable bouillon cubes

Salt and fresh-ground black pepper to taste

QUICK TIP

Some delicious add-ins to this soup are dumplings and left-over baked chicken cut into small pieces. Follow the recipe, and halfway through the process, stir in the baked chicken pieces. When the soup almost is finished cooking, add the dumplings (see dumplings recipe and instructions on page 62).

In a large pot, heat the olive oil over low heat. Add the onion, bell peppers, and celery, stirring occasionally until softened, about 5 minutes.

Stir in the minced garlic and cook for 2 minutes.

Drain the green peas and stir them into the sauté.

Add the broth, bay leaves, bouillon, salt and a few turns of fresh-ground black pepper. Cover and let cook, stirring occasionally, until peas have dissolved, about 35 to 40 minutes.

Remove bay leaves and serve warm.

POTATO, CAULIFLOWER & LEEK SOUP

SERVES ABOUT 6

I put these vegetables into one pot because of my finicky children. One likes cauliflower; the other likes potato and leeks. Rather than making two separate soups, I combined them into one interesting flavor, and it was a palette pleaser. Problem solved!

2   tablespoons olive oil

1   large sweet onion, finely chopped

3   cloves garlic, minced

3   medium-size leeks, thoroughly washed and chopped

1   medium carrot, peeled and finely chopped

2   large russet potatoes, peeled and cubed

1   large head of cauliflower, cut into small pieces (even stems)

Salt and pepper

2   cartons (32 ounces each) chicken or vegetable broth

2   bay leaves

1½ cups milk

Fresh parsley for serving

QUICK TIP

This soup is so creamy and flavorful that you'll never believe you're eating your vegetables!

In a large pot over medium heat, warm the olive oil. Add the onion, garlic, leeks, and carrot. Sauté until soft, about 2 to 3 minutes.

Add the potatoes and cauliflower, then sprinkle with salt and pepper to taste and stir together. Cook for another 5 minutes.

Pour in the chicken or vegetable broth, add the bay leaves, and bring to a boil. Reduce to a simmer and cook for about 20 minutes, until vegetables are tender. Remove the bay leaves and discard.

Using a blender (or an immersion blender) puree the vegetables until smooth.

Pour in the milk and stir together until thoroughly combined. Taste for flavor and add salt and pepper if desired.

If you prefer the soup to have a thinner texture, simply add more milk and puree until desired consistency is reached.

Distribute the soup into separate bowls and top with fresh parsley.

Serve warm and enjoy!

BUTTERNUT SQUASH SOUP
SERVES ABOUT 12

When summer starts to wind down and the cooler temperatures of fall start to set in, this hearty soup is one of the best quick and delicious ways to welcome my favorite time of year.

2 tablespoons olive oil

1 large sweet Vidalia onion, thinly sliced

½ red bell pepper, chopped

½ yellow bell pepper, chopped

2 celery stalks, chopped

4 medium cloves garlic, finely chopped

1 butternut squash (2½ pounds), peeled, seeded, and cut into 1-inch cubes or 1 container of precut butternut squash chunks

1 large carrot, peeled and chopped

4 cups low-sodium chicken or vegetable stock, plus more as needed

1 bay leaf

Kosher salt and fresh-ground black pepper to taste

Fresh parsley, chopped, for garnish

½ cup toasted pumpkin seeds, for garnish (optional)

QUICK TIP

Butternut squash is highly nutritious and a hearty meal. Low in fat, it delivers an ample dose of dietary fiber, making it an exceptionally heart-friendly choice. It provides significant amounts of potassium, important for bone health, and vitamin B6, essential for the proper functioning of both the nervous and immune systems.

In a large pot, heat 2 tablespoons olive oil over medium heat. Add onion, bell peppers, and celery. Stir and cook for 3 minutes and then add the garlic.

Lower heat to medium and cook, stirring, until soft and lightly golden, about 8 minutes. Lower heat as necessary to prevent burning.

Add squash and carrot to the pot and mix well. Add stock and bay leaf.

Cover and bring to a boil, then lower heat and simmer until vegetables are very soft, about 10 minutes. Remove and discard the bay leaf.

Working in batches, puree the soup in a blender, or with an immersion blender, until completely smooth.

Pour soup back into the pot and return to the stove on medium heat. Season with salt and fresh-ground black pepper to taste and simmer for 5 minutes. Thin, if necessary, with additional stock until desired consistency is reached.

Serve soup in warmed bowls and garnish with fresh chopped parsley and toasted pumpkin seeds.

GARDEN TOMATO BASIL SOUP
SERVES 4 TO 6

One summer when I had an abundant harvest of basil from my garden and grew tired of making pesto sauce, I decided to try making tomato basil soup—one that wasn't acidic or thin. So with some modifications of a traditional recipe, I came up with my version of this elegant soup. Every year, when the first feel of fall is in the air, I harvest my basil and make this delicious soup and store it in containers in the freezer. It keeps well through the fall and winter months. I love eating it with a side of flat bread.

2   tablespoons olive oil

1   tablespoon tomato paste

4   garlic cloves, minced

1   large sweet Vidalia onion, medium diced

½   cup yellow bell pepper, medium diced

½   cup red bell pepper, medium diced

2   cans (28 ounces each) peeled tomatoes

1   cup vegetable or chicken broth

1   chicken bouillon cube

1   tablespoon sugar

¼   cup heavy cream

15   basil leaves, roughly chopped

¼   teaspoon dried oregano

½   teaspoon dried pepper flakes

Kosher salt and fresh-ground black pepper to taste

Croutons and grated parmesan cheese for garnish (optional)

In a large soup pot, heat the olive oil over medium heat. Add the tomato paste and cook for about 3 minutes, stirring frequently to avoid burning.

Add garlic, onion, and bell peppers and sauté until translucent and fragrant, about 5 to 7 minutes.

Pour in the tomatoes (including the juice), broth, bouillon and sugar. Bring to a low simmer and cook uncovered for 15 minutes or until the mixture has thickened.

Add the heavy cream, basil, oregano, and red pepper flakes. Season to taste with salt and pepper.

Using an immersion blender (or carefully transfer soup to a blender), puree until there are no large chunks of vegetables left. The mixture should be smooth and creamy.

Stir in the Parmesan cheese to taste, place in soup bowls, and top with croutons, if using. For added elegance and flamboyant taste, garnish with a basil leaf.

Serve hot.

JANEL'S MUSHROOM IN YOUR HEART SOUP
SERVES 4

A recipe of love and friendship boils in this pot of soup that fills me up with content and warmth anytime I have a bowl of it. There was a time when I needed a little compassion and my amazing friend Janel brought me her mushroom soup. Janel's sweet ingredients combined with her loving care make this the perfect combination for soul and tummy filling. The delicate and creaminess of the broth alone can bring brightness to a dull day (just like Janel), and with the chopped parsley garnish, who could resist warming up?

1	tablespoon olive oil	½ to 1	teaspoon fresh-ground black pepper
2	cloves garlic, minced	4	tablespoons butter
¼	teaspoon dried thyme	4	tablespoons flour
¼	cup finely chopped parsley	2	cups chicken broth
2	cups baby bella mushrooms, cleaned and finely chopped	2	cups half and half
1	teaspoon kosher salt		

In a large pot, heat the olive oil. Add the minced garlic, mushrooms, salt, and fresh-ground black pepper. Sauté until the mushrooms have become browned and all of the liquid has evaporated.

Add the butter and flour to the pot, stir, and cook for about 2 minutes. The butter and flour will form a thick paste and coat the mushrooms and bottom of the pot. Be careful not to burn.

Add the chicken broth and dried thyme. Stir well to dissolve all of the flour from the bottom of the pot.

Cover and allow the liquid to come to a simmer. The flour will slightly thicken the broth.

Stir in the half and half. Taste for flavor. Add additional salt and pepper if desired.

Sprinkle with chopped parsley.

Serve hot with slices of warm, crusty bread.

desserts

NO CRY APPLE PIE

MAKES ONE 9-INCH PIE

I am as proud of this pie as I am to be American! Growing up, I had never had apple pie. In fact, apples aren't native and don't grow in Guyana. Of course I knew what an apple was and had tasted this crunchy fruit when it was imported, yet I had no clue it could be turned into pie until I moved to the US. After many years of trial and error, my practice had become progress and now a sought-after dessert item from my kitchen. What makes this delicacy noteworthy is the crust—an ornate pastry in and of itself that will have your guests certain you ordered from a bakery.

Perfect Piecrust (see recipe on page 76)

6 cups golden delicious apples (about 6 medium), peeled and sliced

2 tablespoons orange juice

⅓ cup firmly packed light brown sugar

⅓ cup granulated sugar

3 tablespoons all-purpose flour

1 teaspoon ground cinnamon

¼ teaspoon ground nutmeg

¼ teaspoon kosher salt

2 tablespoons butter

1 to 2 teaspoons milk

1 teaspoon granulated sugar

QUICK TIP

Be gentle with yourself. You aren't in a race for perfection, but with tenderness and with effort you will surely come close!

Preheat oven to 400 F.

On a well-floured board, roll out one disk of piecrust to 9 inches. (You can also roll the crust between waxed paper.) Place the crust into a pie dish and trim the edges. Place the pie shell in the refrigerator while you prepare the filling.

In a large bowl, toss apples and orange juice. Add in the brown sugar, granulated sugar, flour, cinnamon, nutmeg, and salt. Toss until coated.

Remove the pie shell from the refrigerator and spoon the filling into it. Dot with butter. Moisten the pastry edge with water.

Roll out the second disk of piecrust to 9 inches and flip onto the filled pie. Trim the edges, flute or crimp them, and cut slits on the top crust for steam to escape.

Brush the top with milk and sprinkle with the 1 teaspoon sugar. Cover the top with a sheet of nonstick foil to prevent overbrowning.

Bake for 45 minutes. Remove foil and bake 10 to 20 minutes or until apples are tender, filling in center is bubbly, and the crust is golden brown.

Cool pie to room temperature before serving.

KELLIE'S ADDICTIVE CHOCOLATE CAKE
SERVES 10 TO 12

What is sweet, exciting, and lights up my life? That would be my daughter, Kellie—and the cake named for her. When Kellie tried this cake for the first time, she ate almost the whole thing; she could not get enough and claimed, "This cake is addictive," hence the name. Kellie, just like this chocolate ganache-glazed cake, has many sides that absolutely enamor me, from her sense of humour and light-heartedness to the richness of her ideas. I can't get enough of her, and she can't get enough of this cake, and neither will your loved ones.

Dry Ingredients:

1¾ cups all-purpose flour, plus more for dusting pans

2 cups granulated pure cane sugar

¾ cups dutch cocoa powder

1 tablespoon ground flax seed meal

2 teaspoons baking soda

1 teaspoon baking powder

1 teaspoon kosher salt

Wet Ingredients:

1 cup buttermilk, room temperature (shaken)

2 tablespoons sour cream

½ cup canola oil

2 large eggs, room temperature

2 teaspoons pure almond extract

2 teaspoons pure vanilla extract

1 cup freshly brewed hot coffee

Chocolate Buttercream Frosting and Chocolate Ganache (recipes on following pages)

Preheat the oven to 350 F. Spray 2 8-inch round cake pans with nonstick spray and dust them with flour. Then line them with parchment paper.

In the bowl of an electric mixer fitted with a paddle attachment, mix the dry ingredients on low speed until combined.

In another bowl mix the wet ingredients, minus the hot coffee, buttercream, and ganache.

With the mixer on low speed, slowly add the wet ingredients to the dry.

With mixer still on low, add the coffee and stir just to combine, scraping the bottom of the bowl with a rubber spatula.

Pour the batter into prepared pans and bake for 35 to 40 minutes, until a tester inserted in the center comes out clean.

Cool in the pans completely, then remove the cakes from the pans and place on a cooling rack.

To assemble the cake, slice each cake in half and place one piece flat side up on a flat serving plate. With a spatula, spread the top with chocolate buttercream frosting. Place the second layer on top and repeat the process with the third layer. Do not frost the top of the fourth layer.

Brush any loose crumbs from the sides of the cake. Using a cake spatula or knife, cover the sides and top of the cake with a thin layer of the ganache, using only a small amount of the ganache for now.

Refrigerate for 10 minutes and then remove the cake from serving plate and place on a wire rack. Place the wire rack over a large baking sheet to catch any ganache that drips off the cake.

Pour the remaining ganache onto the center of the cake and quickly spread with a large knife or cake spatula using big strokes to push the ganache over the sides of the cake.

Gently place 2 large spatulas under the cake and transfer onto a cake stand or serving plate. Let the ganache set before decorating with fresh berries or piping with extra buttercream frosting.

CHOCOLATE BUTTERCREAM FROSTING

6 ounces semisweet chocolate
(baking bar or chocolate
wafers can be used)

2 sticks unsalted butter at
room temperature

1 teaspoon kosher salt

1¼ cups confectioners' sugar

1 teaspoon pure almond extract

1 tablespoon instant granulated coffee

2 teaspoons hot tap water

Chop the chocolate and place in a heatproof bowl. Bring a medium pot of water to a simmer. Turn off the heat; place the bowl with chocolate on top and gently stir until just melted. Then set aside to cool.

In the bowl of an electric mixer fitted with the paddle attachment, beat the butter and kosher salt on medium speed for 30 seconds. On low speed, slowly add the confectioners' sugar and almond extract, then beat at medium speed, scraping down the bowl until smooth and creamy.

Dissolve the coffee powder in 2 teaspoons hot tap water.

On low speed, add the melted chocolate and coffee to the butter mixture and blend well. Do not let it whip.

CHOCOLATE GANACHE

8 ounces semisweet or bittersweet
chocolate, cut into small pieces
(chocolate wafers may be used)

¾ cup heavy whipping cream

2 tablespoons unsalted butter

1 tablespoon brandy or
orange liqueur (optional)

Place the chopped chocolate in a medium-sized heatproof bowl. Set aside.

Heat the cream and butter in a small saucepan over medium heat. (You can also heat the cream and butter in the microwave.) Bring just to a boil.

Immediately pour the boiling cream over the chocolate and let stand without stirring for 3 minutes.

Stir gently (so as not to incorporate air into the ganache) with a spoon or spatula until smooth. If desired, add the liqueur.

This makes enough ganache to cover a double-layer 8-inch cake or torte.

QUICK TIP

This ganache can be made into chocolate truffles. Cover and refrigerate for 24 hours, roll into small balls, and then roll in desired coating, such as cocoa powder, confectioners' sugar, chopped nuts, or shredded coconut. Then drizzle with melted chocolate to create swirls.

PLUM BLOSSOM CAKE
SERVES 6 TO 8

My daughter Kellie does random acts of kindness to surprise me. This cake was one of her random gifts of love she made for me when I came home from work one evening and, ironically enough, needed a beautiful distraction to my day. She showed me how to make it. Then I added my spin of flavors. I love making it as soon as early summer sets in and black plums are in full bloom at the farmers markets.

½ cup (1 stick) plus 1 tablespoon unsalted butter, plus extra for the pan, at room temperature

4 firm, ripe black plums, washed and each cut into 8 wedges, discard pit

¼ cup plus ⅔ cup (or 10 tablespoons plus 2 teaspoons) granulated sugar

1 cup all-purpose flour

¾ teaspoon baking powder

¼ teaspoon baking soda

¼ teaspoon kosher salt

¼ teaspoon ground cardamom

1 large egg

⅔ cup sour cream

1 teaspoon pure almond extract

1 teaspoon pure vanilla extract

Heat oven to 350 F. Butter an 8-inch round cake pan and line the bottom with parchment paper.

In a large skillet over medium-high heat, melt 1 tablespoon of the butter. Add the plums and ¼ cup of the sugar and cook, tossing, until the sugar dissolves and the juices from the plums become syrupy, 3 to 4 minutes. Do not overcook.

Arrange the plums in the cake pan in slightly overlapping concentric circles, starting from the outside. Spoon any pan juices over the top.

In a small bowl, whisk together the flour, baking powder, baking soda, salt, and cardamom.

In a separate bowl and with an electric mixer, beat the remaining ½ cup butter and ⅔ cup sugar until fluffy. Beat in the egg, sour cream, and almond and vanilla extracts. Gradually add the flour mixture, mixing just until incorporated.

Pour the batter over the plums and bake until a toothpick inserted in the center comes out clean, 50 to 55 minutes. Let cool in the pan for 1 hour.

Place a large plate over the cake pan and invert the cake onto the plate.

Serve at room temperature with scoops of frozen vanilla yogurt.

PERFECT PIECRUST

MAKES ONE DOUBLE PIECRUST

For a long time I have been on a quest to find a pastry crust that I can call "perfect." After many tries, research, and measurements, I finally conquered what I called "finding the perfect piecrust."

2½ cups all-purpose flour, spooned and leveled

1 teaspoon salt

1 teaspoon pure granulated sugar

2 sticks (16 tablespoons) *cold,* unsalted butter, cut into cubes

½ cup ice water, divided

QUICK TIP

To prevent your piecrust from shrinking while it's baking, refrigerate it for 40 minutes or freeze for 20 minutes after you've rolled it out.

In a food processor, combine the flour, salt, and sugar and pulse to mix. Add the butter and pulse until the mixture resembles coarse meal with just a few pea-size pieces of butter remaining.

Add ¼ cup ice water and pulse until the dough starts to get crumbly, add the other ¼ cup water and continue to pulse. The dough should hold together when squeezed with fingers. To ensure a flaky crust, do not overwork the dough.

Divide the dough in half and wrap each piece in plastic wrap. Refrigerate until firm, at least 1 hour before use.

ORANGE CHOCOLATE CURLS CAKE

SERVES 6

The flavors of oranges and dark chocolate come together decadently in this cake. The silent presence of ginger adds a pop that makes one wonder, *Hmmmm, what is that exotic burst of flavor?*

For the Cake:

1½ cups cake flour

¼ teaspoon baking powder

¼ teaspoon baking soda

½ teaspoon kosher salt

¼ teaspoon ground ginger

3 ounces (6 tablespoons) freshly squeezed orange juice, divided

3 ounces (6 tablespoons) buttermilk, room temperature

1 teaspoon pure vanilla extract

2 teaspoons pure orange extract

1 teaspoon almond extract

½ cup (1 stick) unsalted butter, room temperature

1½ cups granulated sugar, divided

2 tablespoons sour cream

2 extra-large eggs, room temperature

2 tablespoons plus 2 teaspoons grated orange zest (3 oranges)

8-ounce dark chocolate bar (optional)

For the Orange Buttercream Icing:

2 sticks unsalted butter, room temperature (not too soft)

1 teaspoon kosher salt

1½ tablespoons freshly squeezed orange juice

1 teaspoon orange extract

1¼ cups confectioners' sugar, sifted

Heat the oven to 350 F. Grease an 8-inch round cake pan and line the bottom with parchment paper.

In a large bowl, sift together the flour, baking powder, baking soda, salt, and ground ginger. Set aside.

In another bowl, combine 3 tablespoons of the orange juice with the buttermilk and vanilla, orange, and almond extracts. Set aside.

In the bowl of an electric mixer fitted with the paddle attachment, cream the butter and 1 cup of the granulated sugar for about 5 minutes or until light and fluffy. Scrape down the sides, add the sour cream, and mix well.

With the mixer on medium speed, beat in the eggs one at a time.

Add the orange zest. Add the flour and buttermilk mixtures alternately, beginning and ending with the flour.

Pour the batter into the pan, smooth the top, and bake for 45 to 50 minutes or when a tester inserted into the center comes out clean.

While the cake bakes, cook the remaining ½ cup of granulated sugar with the remaining 3 tablespoons orange juice in a small saucepan over low heat until the sugar dissolves.

When the cake is done, let it cool for 10 minutes. Remove from the pan and place it on a baking rack set over a tray. Spoon the orange syrup over the cake and cool completely before icing.

Prepare the icing while the cake cools. In an electric mixer fitted with the paddle attachment, add the butter, kosher salt, orange juice, and orange extract and mix to combine. Slowly add the sifted confectioners' sugar and mix until smooth. Do not whip.

When the cake is completely cool, place it on a cake stand or serving plate. Place a generous amount of icing on top and push down to sides to cover the cake completely. Add more icing as needed. Smooth the cake with a cake spatula.

Decorate the top with chocolate curls and additional orange zest if you like. To create the chocolate curls, over parchment paper carefully pull a vegetable peeler across the broad surface of the bar of dark chocolate. This works best if the chocolate is at room temperature. For narrower curls, use the side of the bar.

MOM'S FABULOUS BLACK CAKE (RUM CAKE)

MAKES TWO 8-INCH CAKES

My mom is well known for her amazing black cake! Famous for its uniquely dense texture, dark color, and rich and robust taste, it is the most requested treat by friends and family. The steps are worth the while to make and enjoy this delicious dessert.

At first glance, it resembles a chocolate cake, but the deep, dark color comes from the main ingredient—dried, macerated fruits. Prunes, currants, raisins, and glacé cherries are chopped finely then soaked in port wine and dark rum for months to years on end. This fruit mixture is always present in my mother's pantry. When making black cake, the mixture is added to the batter along with aromatic flavorings and warm spices.

Making it reminds me of Christmas holidays in South America and one year in particular when my favorite aunt, Lyennie, along with my brother, cousin, and I pretended to be my parents having fun at a holiday party. We ended up eating the cakes my mom had made to share. Luckily, we didn't get into trouble, but she had to make another set of cakes. My dear aunt is no longer with us, but I like to think she's looking down from the skies and sharing the laughter too. It's interesting how food is a fixture for memories.

For the Macerated Fruits:

1   pound prunes, pitted

1   pound raisins

1   pound currants

8   ounces candied (glacé) red cherries

4   ounces mixed, candied fruit peel

3   cups port wine

3   cups plain or dark rum

For the Burnt Sugar:

1   teaspoon vegetable shortening

2   cups dark brown sugar

5   whole cloves

2   cinnamon sticks

½   cup port wine or any red table wine

For the Cake Batter:

1   cup (2 sticks) unsalted butter, room temperature

1   tablespoon vegetable shortening

3   tablespoons vegetable oil

2   cups brown sugar

5   large eggs, room temperature

3   teaspoons vanilla extract

3   teaspoons almond extract

1   teaspoon ground nutmeg

1   teaspoon ground cinnamon

1½ cups macerated fruits

½   cup walnuts, chopped

2   cups all-purpose flour

¾   cup burnt sugar

Candied red cherries, chopped

½   cup plain or spiced rum or 1 cup port wine (optional)

Prepare the macerated fruits well in advance.

In a large bowl, combine all of the fruits and mix well. Using a food processor or blender on medium speed, add the fruits a little at a time with enough wine to chop the fruits into a paste. Repeat the process until the fruits are mashed and juicy. The mixture should not be too watery. Transfer the mixture to a container and add rum. Stir and cover. Let the fruits soak at minimum one week or even one year, adding more wine periodically.

Prepare the burnt sugar before making the cake.

Grease a large pot with the shortening, then add the sugar, cloves, and cinnamon sticks and place over low heat. The sugar will start to caramelize. Once dark brown, pour in the wine slowly. The mixture will start to bubble. Cook until the sugar is completely melted and has no grains and a texture that resembles honey. Remove the pot from the heat and discard cloves and cinnamon sticks. Let cool completely. Once cool, taste for flavor. It should not be bitter, or this will ruin the cake.

Now you're ready to make the cake.

Preheat the oven to 325 F. Spray two 8-inch round cake pans with nonstick cooking spray and line with parchment paper.

In an electric mixer fitted with the paddle attachment, cream the butter, shortening, vegetable oil, and sugar until light and fluffy, about 8 minutes.

Add eggs one at a time, mixing well after each addition.

Add vanilla and almond extracts and mix well.

Add nutmeg and cinnamon.

Mix in the preserved fruits and chopped nuts.

Turn the mixer off and fold in the flour. Add 5 tablespoons burnt sugar at a time until a dark color is achieved. Mix well.

Divide the batter among the two cake pans.

Sprinkle the chopped candid cherries on top and bake for 50 to 55 minutes. When done, a cake tester or long tooth pick will come out clean when inserted in the middle. Do not over bake.

Remove the cakes from the oven and pour rum or port wine over them. After removing cake from oven, it may seem it is under cooked. Do not be alarmed as this is how it is supposed to be. After 2 to 3 days the texture will change.

Let cool completely in the pans.

Cover the pans loosely with plastic wrap and allow the cakes to absorb the rum or wine at least overnight but ideally for 2 or no more than 3 days for heightened flavor.

Serve with hot coffee or tea.

QUICK TIP

Store in a tightly closed container at room temperature for up to two weeks to maintain moist and fragrant flavors. Refrigerate for longer storage, up to 6 months.

MANGO MOUSSE

SERVES ABOUT 15

Have you ever had a moose for dinner? Don't be silly; we have that for dessert! Although I was very familiar with mango, my neighbor introduced me to mango mousse, and both the mousse and my neighbor have become a part of my heart. This delightful indulgence brings new life to mango and is a perfect conversation piece. After all, there's a mousse at your table! Make it and seek new friends to share it with. I'm glad I did.

- 1 package (8 ounces) cream cheese
- 3 packets (sachets) unflavored gelatin
- 2½ cups cold water
- 3 cups milk, divided (whole or 2%)
- 1 can (30 ounces) mango pulp
- 2 cups plus 4 tablespoons pure cane sugar
- 1 package (8 ounces) Cool Whip, plain flavor
- Fresh mango slices for garnish (optional)

Open the cream cheese and let come to room temperature.

Dissolve the gelatin in the cold water for 15 minutes.

After 15 minutes and once the gelatin solidifies, pour in ¼ cup of the milk and heat in microwave for 40 seconds until the gelatin melts completely.

In a blender, combine the mango pulp, gelatin mixture, remaining milk, cream cheese, and sugar. (Depending on the size of your blender, you may have to do this in two batches.) Blend to a very smooth texture.

Pour the mixture into a big bowl and whisk in the Cool Whip until it dissolves. Taste for sweetness, add more sugar if desired.

Pour the mixture into a large casserole dish, rectangular dish, or into ramekins. The amount poured in should be about a medium height of thickness, about 3 inches.

Cover and refrigerate for 24 hours to set.

Garnish with fresh mango slices and serve.

RICE PUDDING (KHEER)

SERVES 8

- ½ cup white basmati rice
- 12 cups milk (whole or 2%)
- ⅔ cup sugar
- ½ teaspoon ground cardamom
- ½ teaspoon ground nutmeg
- 1 cinnamon stick
- 5 whole cloves
- 2 teaspoons vanilla extract
- 4 teaspoons almond extract
- 5 tablespoons raisins
- 4 tablespoons sliced cashews, optional

Wash the rice thoroughly with water then place in a large, deep pot.

Add the milk, sugar, spices, extracts, and raisins. Stir well.

Cover and bring to a boil.

Lower the heat and cook, gently boiling, for about 1 hour or until the rice is thoroughly cooked and soft and the milk has thickened to a thick pudding consistency. Taste for level of sweetness. Add more sugar if desired.

Remove and discard the cinnamon stick and whole cloves.

When ready to serve, garnish with sliced cashews.

QUICK TIP

There are a few ways to modify this delicious dessert. For instance, I enjoy eating it warm. To enjoy cold, chill for 4 hours before serving. If you prefer almonds to cashews, garnish with almonds. To take it up a notch for an adult tasting, mix in 1 tablespoon brandy or rum.

VERMICELLI BARS
SERVES 12

- 4 tablespoons butter (½ stick)
- 1 package (17 ounces) vermicelli noodles
- 1 can (14 ounces) sweetened condensed milk
- 2 cups water, more if needed
- 1 tablespoon almond extract
- 1 teaspoon vanilla extract
- ½ teaspoon ground cinnamon
- ¼ teaspoon ground nutmeg
- ⅓ teaspoon ground cardamom
- 1 cinnamon stick
- ¼ cup raisins, yellow or black
- 15 maraschino cherries or ¼ cup candied red cherries, roughly chopped
- Chopped pistachios or cashew halves (optional)

In a deep pot on low heat, melt the butter. Add the vermicelli noodles and toast until some of the noodles become lightly brown. This will happen fast, so do not walk away from the stove.

When most of the noodles are brown, add the condensed milk, water, extracts, spices, and raisins.

Keeping the stove on low heat, let the noodles cook in the milk mixture until they start to soften up. If the liquid is absorbed and the noodles are still firm, add a little more water. About 15 minutes in, the mixture should start to clump together. (Everyone's stove temperature is different, so if it has not reached this stage as yet, just wait until it starts to look like a really thick pudding).

Don't let the mixture be too dried out; if it coats the back of a spoon thickly without dripping, then remove from heat and remove and discard the cinnamon stick.

Add the chopped cherries and optional nuts and stir to combine.

Pour into a serving dish that will allow your vermicelli to be about 1½ inches in thickness. Let this rest at room temperature for about 1 hour to firm up.

Cut into squares and enjoy.

SHORTBREAD COOKIES
YIELDS ABOUT 24 3-INCH SHAPED COOKIES

I find this recipe very useful. Not only is it quick and easy to make, but also I like its versatility. It can be used for cut-out cookies, thumbprint cookies, and free-form style cookies where you can add in toppings of your choice—nuts, sprinkles, chocolate chips, or ginger chips. The texture of the cookies will never disappoint.

¾ pound (3 sticks) unsalted butter, room temperature

1 cup granulated sugar, more for sprinkling

2 tablespoons almond extract

1 teaspoon vanilla extract

1 teaspoon rose water

Zest of one lemon

1 teaspoon lemon juice

3½ cups all-purpose flour

¼ teaspoon kosher salt

In an electric mixer fitted with the paddle attachment, cream together the butter and sugar until just combined, about 5 minutes. Scrape down the sides of the bowl and then add the extracts, rose water, lemon zest, and lemon juice and mix again.

Separately, combine the flour and salt.

With the mixer on low speed, add the flour mixture to the creamed butter and sugar. Mix until the dough starts to come together.

Place on a floured board and roll together. Divide into two disks, wrap in plastic, and chill for 35 to 40 minutes.

When ready to bake, preheat the oven to 350 F and line cookie sheets with parchment paper.

Roll out the dough to about ½ inch thick and cut into desired shaped cookies.

Place on cookie sheets and lightly sprinkle with extra granulated sugar. Bake for 14 to 16 minutes until the edges turn slightly brown. Remove from the oven and let sit for about 3 minutes and then move the cookies onto a rack to cool.

Decorate with icing or melt chocolate and dip half of the cookies into the melted chocolate and let dry.

BANANA FRITTERS

MAKES ABOUT 30

Growing up I learned not to waste food. Something as simple as over-ripe bananas were turned into delicious and healthy snack bites. Whenever the bananas ripened to the occasion, my mom turned them into after-school snacks. I now use them as great mid-morning or afternoon snacks. Enjoy with a delicious cup of hot tea or coffee or serve them as an exotic dessert for simple entertaining.

2 ripened bananas, peeled	¼ cup raisins
⅔ cup granulated sugar	3 cups all-purpose flour
1 teaspoon baking powder	Oil for frying
¾ teaspoon yeast	Confectioners' sugar (optional)
¼ teaspoon ground cinnamon	
¼ teaspoon ground nutmeg	
½ teaspoon vanilla extract	

QUICK TIP

The key factor here is the oil temperature. If it's too low, the batter will absorb a lot of the oil, so make sure the oil is warm enough. If it's too hot, the fritters will be raw. Do a test by frying one fritter before adding the rest. This step will give you an idea of the oil temperature.

In a medium bowl, mash the bananas with a fork or potato masher.

Stir in the sugar and mix well until it dissolves.

Add the baking powder and yeast. Stir to combine.

Add the cinnamon, nutmeg, vanilla, and raisins and mix well. Stir in the flour and mix well to the consistency of a creamy batter.

Cover and let batter double in size, about 15 minutes.

Using a large skillet or cast iron pan, add oil up to ½ inch deep and heat over medium heat.

Using a metal spoon (eating spoon), scoop the batter into rounds and fry in batches, turning until golden brown, about 5 minutes. Do not overcrowd the pan—this will create soggy fritters and absorb excess oil.

Using a slotted spoon, remove and drain the fritters and place them on paper towels. Sprinkle with confectioners' sugar if desired.

Serve warm.

MOORE CUSTARD, PLEASE

SERVES 8

The eggy cousin to pudding is custard, and it's an all-time favorite dessert dish in Guyana, England, and now in your house! Custard is easy to make, light, and not too sweet. What makes this version of custard unique is the addition of cardamom. I am in love with cardamom for many reasons: its distinct flavor, the almost infinite health benefits, and its simple yet elegant addition to the visual presentation. Just like the Moore family does, everyone will be asking you for more!

8 eggs	¼ teaspoon ground cinnamon
2 cans (12 ounces each) evaporated milk	¼ teaspoon ground nutmeg, plus more for sprinkling
7 tablespoons pure cane sugar	⅓ teaspoon cardamom
1 tablespoon almond extract	Hot water for water bath
1 teaspoon vanilla extract	

QUICK TIP

Fun fact: cardamom, a staple in Ayurvedic medicine, is known as the "Queen of Spices."

Preheat the oven to 350 F.

Spray 8 dessert ramekins (or a medium-size, deep baking dish) with nonstick spray and then place them in a large, deep baking pan to pour water in.

In a large bowl, whisk the eggs.

Add the evaporated milk and beat well.

Add the sugar, extracts, cinnamon, nutmeg, and cardamom and continue whisking to combine. Taste for flavor. Add more sugar or spices if desired.

Slowly pour the mixture into the sprayed ramekins or baking dish.

Lightly sprinkle tops of the custard with some nutmeg.

Carefully pour the hot water into the large pan about ½ way up the baking dish to create a water bath.

Place in the oven and bake for 20 to 25 minutes. The texture should be slightly jiggly as it will set when cooled. Do not overcook.

Remove from the oven and let cool before serving.

This dessert is best enjoyed at room temperature. Refrigerate any leftovers.

holiday
classics

TURKEY-DAY TURKEY & GRAVY

SERVES 8-10

When we first migrated to the US, my brother and I heard some shocking stories about the procedures involved in cooking a turkey. We laugh today at the lengths our imaginations took us as we heard our friends and folk describe their fear in putting together and roasting this truly iconic dish in American culture. "It takes how long?!" No wonder turkey is on reserve for one day a year, Thanksgiving, when the family chef has all day to season, baste, and monitor.

When I got married, I took on the turkey challenge to satisfy my curiosity. I researched the steps to "cooking a perfect turkey." My first two tries weren't bad, and I soon realized a turkey does not require getting up at 4 a.m. to put it in the oven for dinner at 5 p.m. Thanksgiving is especially special in my family as we remember each year our initial distress around this delicious tradition and how we solved the mystery of cooking a roasted turkey.

For the Acid Bath:

2   large lemons

¼   cup white vinegar

15-20 pound turkey (fresh or frozen)

For the Brine:

1   cup kosher salt

1½ cups granulated sugar

½   cup molasses

½   cup low-sodium soy sauce

¼   cup whole peppercorns

¼   cup whole allspice

5   dried bay leaves

1   sprig of fresh rosemary

1   sprig of fresh thyme

3   quarts (12 cups) water

3   quarts (12 cups) ice cubes

Brining bag

For the Sage Butter:

8   ounces (1 stick) salted butter

2   tablespoons olive oil

2   teaspoons herbes de Provence

5   sage leaves, medium chopped

For the Turkey and Gravy:

1   orange, quartered

2   sprigs fresh rosemary

1   small bunch of fresh thyme

1   bunch of fresh sage, divided evenly

3   dried bay leaves

Sweet paprika

Nonstick foil

Butcher's twine

Large turkey-size oven-roasting bag

Nonstick cooking spray

1   tablespoon flour

Corn starch

Fresh-ground black pepper

Give the turkey an acid bath.

In South America, all meats and fish are cleaned well before cooking to kill or remove bacteria. Acids may or may not be effective in killing bacteria (I'll leave that to the scientists to debate), but they definitely tenderize the meat and create pathways for marinade, or brine in the case of this turkey, to penetrate the meat and infuse it with flavor.

Fill a very large bowl with cool tap water, squeeze the lemons, add the juice and rinds and the ¼ cup vinegar, and then place the turkey in the bowl and let it sit for about ½ hour. (Do not let it sit any longer, or the acid could make the meat tough.) Rinse well and drain before moving the turkey to the brining bag.

Brine the turkey.

In a large pot, combine all of the ingredients, *except* the ice cubes. Place on the stove, heat, and stir until the sugar and salt dissolve and then add ice cubes. Let the mixture cool completely.

Place a big turkey-size brining bag in a large, deep tray or bowl. Place the turkey breast side down in the brining bag.

Pour the cool brine mixture over the turkey. Seal tightly, so the brine does not spill out. Brine for 12 hours in the refrigerator or a cooler filled with ice.

Roast the turkey.

Preheat the oven to 350 F.

Prepare the sage butter. In a small pot, melt the butter and then add the olive oil, herbes de Provence, and half of the chopped sage. Heat for 1 minute. Stir well. Set aside.

Remove the turkey from the brine and discard the brine. Pat the turkey dry.

Fill the cavity with orange slices, rosemary sprigs, thyme, remaining sage, and bay leaves. Brush the entire bird with melted sage butter. Sprinkle the skin with sweet paprika. Cover the breast and wings lightly with nonstick foil to prevent over browning or burning. Tie the legs together with butcher's twine.

Spray the insides of a roasting bag with nonstick cooking spray, add 1 tablespoon flour, and shake the bag to distribute the flour. Place the turkey in the bag. Spray the top and sides of the turkey lightly with cooking spray to avoid any sticking. Close the bag with twist tie. Cut 2 to 3 slits on the top and sides of the bag to allow steam to escape.

Place the bagged turkey in a deep roasting pan with a large roasting rack in. Cook for 3½ hours.

Remove the pan from the oven, slowly cut the bag open, and carefully slide it off without removing the turkey skin. At this point the juices will pour into the roasting pan. Carefully pour the juice into a pot and set aside to make gravy.

Return the turkey to the oven and brown until golden, about 10 to 15 minutes depending on your oven. A meat thermometer inserted in the thickest part of the thigh without touching bone should read 165 F. Do not over cook!

Remove from the oven, tent the turkey with aluminum foil, and let rest for about 1 hour before slicing.

Prepare the gravy.

Strain the roasting pan juices into a medium pot and discard all the solids. Spoon off the fat that has risen to the top of the pan juices.

Remove 2 tablespoons of the juices and set aside in a small bowl. Reserve another tablespoon for the stuffing (see recipe on page 91).

continued on following page

continued from previous page

Place the pot on medium heat and simmer pan juices for 5 minutes. Add ½ teaspoon of cornstarch to the 2 tablespoons of pan juices and dissolve and then whisk the mixture into the pan juices, stirring to combine and preventing any lumps from forming.

The gravy will start to thicken. Taste for desired flavor and season to taste, adding fresh-ground black pepper if needed.

Pour into a gravy boat when ready to serve.

Over the years as I continued to add and improve on my Thanksgiving dinner ideas, my children and husband would each say what they liked most and wanted each year. So eventually, I came up with a menu that we all agreed we must have every year. I thought I would share it with you either to choose from or to encourage you to create your own menu using favorites from your family. I've also created a shopping list so that I do not forget any items when it's time to purchase the ingredients. I mean, can you imagine picking up all the ingredients except for the turkey? Yikes!

Thanksgiving Dinner Menu:

Turkey-Day Turkey & Gravy (page 88)
Roasted garlic mashed potatoes
Ren's Macaroni Casserole (page 40)
Scrumptious Stuffing (page 91)
Candied yams
Homemade Cranberry sauce (page 91)
Stir-fry asparagus
Sweet whole kernel corn
Cheddar biscuits
Pumpkin pie
No Cry Apple Pie (page 72)
Pumpkin pecan pie
Wine
Apple cider
Water
Coffee

Shopping List:

Turkey	Cinnamon	Brown sugar	Chicken broth
Yams	Nutmeg	Granulated	Cream of
Walnuts	Cloves	sugar	mushroom soup
Pecans	Ginger	Sage	Oranges
Asparagus	Cardamom,	Thyme	Apples
Corn	ground	Rosemary	
Fresh cranberries	and whole	Garlic	
Stuffing mix	Allspice	Yukon gold	
Pumpkin pie puree	Molasses	potatoes	
Wine	Low-sodium	Red pepper	
Apple cider	soy sauce	Celery	

HOMEMADE CRANBERRY SAUCE

SERVES 8

The first time I tasted cranberry sauce, it was from a can. When I saw it being poured from the can I thought, "Ugh, that is a glob," and of course I didn't like it. Making my own sauce was another of my Thanksgiving accomplishments.

1   12-ounce bag of fresh cranberries, washed and drained

2   cups granulated sugar

⅓   cup water

1   cinnamon stick

3   whole cloves

½   teaspoon ground allspice

¼   teaspoon ground nutmeg

1   orange, zest and juice

In a medium pot, combine the cranberries, sugar, and water. Stir to blend. Bring the mixture to a boil over medium heat.

Reduce to a simmer and add the cinnamon stick, cloves, allspice, and nutmeg. Mix well and let continue to simmer for 5 to 7 minutes. Some of the cranberries will burst and some will remain whole.

Add the orange zest and juice and stir.

Remove from heat, remove cinnamon stick and cloves, and let cool before serving.

SCRUMPTIOUS STUFFING

SERVES 8

When it comes to "stuffings" I like a simple but scrumptious one. It must not be dry, soggy or oily. I've experienced some of those textures during my tastings. I make mine very easy and uncomplicated. I use packaged stuffing mix with my spin of ingredients.

1   tablespoon olive oil

1   celery stalk, diced small

½   cup red bell peppers, diced small

2   sage leaves, chopped

Vegetable, chicken, or turkey broth (see stuffing mix box for quantity of liquid)

1   box stuffing mix of your choice

2   tablespoons cream of mushroom soup

1   tablespoon turkey pan juice (from recipe on page 89)

3   teaspoons flat-leaf parsley, finely chopped for garnish

In a medium pot, heat the olive oil. Add the diced celery and bell peppers and sauté until softened, about 3 minutes. Add the chopped sage.

Following the instructions on the box of stuffing mix, substitute water with the broth and pour the required amount into the pot.

Add the cream of mushroom soup and turkey pan juice. Let mixture simmer.

Add the stuffing mix, stir, and cover.

Remove the pot from the heat and let rest. After 5 minutes, remove the lid and add the chopped parsley. Stir with a fork, then transfer the mixture to a casserole dish. Cover with aluminum foil and bake in a preheated 350 F oven for 10 minutes. Remove from oven and serve warm.

ROASTED CHICKEN & CHIPS
SERVES 5 TO 6

When I arrived to the country I now call home, the US, I was so excited to do everything American, including eating fast food! McDonald's was such a treat. The first time I went to place an order, I said to the employee, "I'd like a Big Mac and chips." This comment perplexed the employee and everyone around me. I soon came to realize that chips have a different meaning in Guyana than they do in the US.

Chips in this recipe are homemade french fries and are a hit all around. Roasted chicken was and still is my favorite dish, and chips are the perfect companion. The fragrance of the roasted chicken brings me right back to sitting at the table with my father, mother, and brother claiming the wings before anyone else could. On Boxing Day (the day after Christmas), this is what we have for dinner.

For the Chicken:

3 to 5 pound whole chicken

5   large carrots, peeled and cut lengthwise

1   large onion, sliced

½   stick salted butter

2   teaspoons herbes de Provence

Kosher salt

Sweet paprika

Creole seasoning

Adobo all-purpose seasoning

Poultry seasoning

Fresh-ground black pepper

2   bay leaves

Thyme, rosemary, and sage sprigs

1   head of garlic, cut in half

1   lemon, cut in quarters

For the Chips:

5   russet potatoes, peeled and sliced julienne (like French fries)

1   cup canola or vegetable oil for frying

Coarse sea salt

Preheat the oven to 400 F.

Remove giblets packet from the bird's cavity and discard. You will not be using them in this recipe. Place the carrots and onions in a roasting pan.

Melt the butter then stir in the herbes de Provence.

Season the insides of the chicken cavity with kosher salt, sweet paprika, creole seasoning, adobo seasoning, poultry seasoning, and pepper. Use your own judgment on how much.

Stuff the chicken with the bay leaves, thyme, rosemary, sage, garlic, and lemon. Tie the legs together with kitchen twine and cover the wing tips with pieces of foil to prevent burning.

Generously sprinkle and rub more creole seasoning and adobo seasoning on the entire chicken, including lifting the skin of the breast area to season the meat. Sprinkle all over with sweet paprika.

Place the chicken on top of the bed of vegetables in the roasting pan. Spoon the melted butter mixture over the bird and roast for 1½ to 1¾ hours.

Make a small cut between the thighs to check for doneness. If juice runs clear, it is finished. Remove from the oven and let rest for 1 hour before carving. Remove the carrots and strain the gravy. Then serve with the chicken.

While the chicken is resting, prepare the chips. Place the sliced potatoes in a bowl of cold, salted water for 15 minutes. Drain and pat dry on a paper towel or kitchen towel.

Heat the oil in a large skillet over medium-high heat. Carefully place potato slices into the hot oil. Fry until golden brown and crispy. Remove and drain on paper towels. Immediately sprinkle with coarse sea salt and mix well to coat.

Serve immediately with roasted chicken and ketchup for dipping.

SPRING STEAKS (LAMB)
SERVES 6-8

My twist on traditional lamb chops turned these steaks into the acclaimed choice for my family. They are delicious when served with roasted garlic mashed potatoes and asparagus. It has become a staple for our Easter dinner.

8 lamb shoulder steaks

⅓ cup Worcestershire sauce (recommend Lea & Perrins)

½ cup soy sauce

½ cup olive oil plus 2 tablespoons

4 tablespoons brown sugar

4 cloves garlic, minced

2 tablespoons fresh rosemary, finely chopped

5 to 6 mint leaves, finely chopped

2 teaspoons fresh thyme, finely chopped

1 teaspoon grated ginger

3 to 4 teaspoons adobo all-purpose seasoning

2 teaspoons herbes de Provence

Fresh-ground black pepper

3 to 4 cups beef or vegetable broth

¼ cup ketchup

1 whole sweet Vidalia onion sliced in rings

1 whole red bell pepper sliced lengthwise

QUICK TIP

For faster cooking, use a pressure cooker to cook the steaks. First, heat the pressure cooker to medium heat and then add 1 tablespoon olive oil and braise the steaks on both sides until nice brown edges are formed. Then add the broth and cook for 15 minutes. Let rest 10 minutes and then carefully let out the steam and remove the steaks from the pot to rest in a platter. Continue the steps above for finishing up the steaks.

Place the lamb in a large bowl or casserole dish.

In a bowl, combine the Worcestershire sauce, soy sauce, ½ cup olive oil, brown sugar, garlic, rosemary, mint, thyme, ginger, adobo seasoning, herbes de Provence, and 3 to 5 turns of fresh-ground black pepper. Whisk well to combine, then pour over the steaks and massage the marinade into the steaks. Cover and refrigerate overnight or 5 hours before cooking.

Bring the meat to room temperature.

Preheat oven to 375 F and line a deep baking dish with foil.

Remove the steaks from the marinade and place in the baking dish. Pour broth over the steaks. Cover with foil and bake for 2 hours, checking for meat tenderness after 1 hour. After you've achieved desired tenderness, remove from the oven and let rest.

In a large frying pan, heat 2 tablespoons olive oil to medium heat. Carefully transfer a few steaks to the frying pan and sear while brushing with ketchup. Brown the steaks on both sides. Arrange the steaks in a serving dish. Continue the process with remaining steaks.

After searing the steaks, using the same pan, toss in the sliced onions and peppers and sauté until tender but don't over cook, about 2 minutes. Layer on top of the steaks and serve.

just eat • party favs

party favs

CARIBBEAN WINGS
SERVES ABOUT 6

½ habanero pepper, seeded and chopped

2 tablespoons soy sauce

2 tablespoons Worcestershire sauce

2 tablespoons honey

2 tablespoons packed light brown sugar

1 tablespoon granulated sugar

1 teaspoon fennel seeds

1 teaspoon cayenne pepper

1 teaspoon ground allspice

1 teaspoon ground turmeric

1 teaspoon dried thyme

1 teaspoon ground ginger

3 cloves garlic, chopped

2 scallions, chopped

2 tablespoons apple cider vinegar

2 tablespoons pineapple juice

2 tablespoons fresh lime juice

2 tablespoons fresh orange juice

3 pounds chicken wings

Green onions, thinly sliced for garnish

Combine the habanero, soy sauce, honey, sugars, fennel seeds, cayenne, allspice, turmeric, thyme, ginger, garlic and scallions in a blender. Add the vinegar, pineapple juice, lime juice, and orange juice and blend until smooth.

Place the wings in a large bowl and pour the marinade over them. Cover with plastic wrap and refrigerate overnight or for 6 to 8 hours.

Preheat the oven to 350 F. Line 2 baking sheets with nonstick foil. Remove the wings from the bowl, place on the lined sheets, and bake 20 minutes.

Pour the marinade in a small saucepan over medium heat and cook until reduced by ⅓, about 10 minutes.

Remove the wings from the oven and brush with the glaze.

Raise the oven temperature to 400 F and continue baking for 15 minutes.

Remove from the oven, turn the wings over, and glaze again. Return to the oven and continue baking until the wings are cooked through, about 5 minutes more.

Place the wings on a serving tray and sprinkle with sliced green onions.

STUFFED (DEVILED) EGGS
SERVES 5 TO 6

Quite often, I get questions and compliments about my deviled eggs. People ask how I make them because they are delicious and addictive. I don't do anything fancy except for making them the way I learned growing up (where we called them "stuffed eggs") and helping my mother. There, we used a very small piece of hot pepper along with the celery leaf as the garnish. That combination gave a burst of exquisite flavors.

6   large, hard-boiled eggs, peeled and sliced in half

¼   cup butter, room temperature

1   tablespoon mayonnaise

1 to 2 teaspoons Dijon mustard

Salt and pepper to taste

Sweet paprika to taste

1   red bell pepper, diced small

Celery leaves

WHY ARE THEY CALLED "DEVILED" EGGS?

In cooking, "to devil" means to chop up food very finely and mix it with hot seasoning or sauce. Hot ... devil ... get it?

Slice the eggs in half lengthwise. Remove the yolks to a medium bowl and place the whites on a serving platter.

Mash the yolks into a fine crumble using a fork. Add the softened butter, mayonnaise, mustard, salt, and pepper and mix well. Taste for desired flavor.

Evenly disperse heaping teaspoons of the yolk mixture into the egg whites. Sprinkle lightly with sweet paprika.

Garnish by gently inserting one piece of celery leaf and one piece of diced bell pepper on top of each egg.

Cover lightly and refrigerate. Bring to room temperature before serving.

REN'S JERK CHICKEN
SERVES ABOUT 6 TO 8

½ cup mild or hot jerk seasoning

2 teaspoons creole seasoning

2 teaspoons kosher salt

2 teaspoons adobo seasoning

1 teaspoon ground allspice

3 teaspoons soy sauce

5 cloves garlic, minced

½ sweet onion, chopped

2 tablespoons softened butter

8 to 10 chicken thighs, skinless with bone
(the bone helps to keep the moisture)

In a large bowl, whisk all of the ingredients except the chicken.

Add the chicken to the marinade and toss to coat well.

Cover and refrigerate overnight or for at least 5 hours.

Let chicken stand at room temperature for 45 minutes.

Preheat the oven to 350 F.

Line a deep baking dish with nonstick foil. Arrange thighs, cover with foil, and bake for 30 minutes.

Remove the pan from the oven, turn the chicken, return it to the oven, and continue baking uncovered for 20 minutes.

Turn the chicken once again and cook for about 5 to 7 minutes more until nicely browned.

Remove from the oven, cover, and let sit for about 20 minutes before serving.

PARTY PASTA
SERVES 12

1 pound tricolor pasta, cooked and drained

1 red bell pepper, thinly sliced lengthwise

1 yellow bell pepper, thinly sliced lengthwise

1 orange bell pepper, thinly sliced lengthwise

1 cup whole cherry tomatoes

2 cups sliced black olives

Crushed red pepper flakes to taste

Salt and fresh-ground black pepper to taste

½ to 1 cup Italian dressing

In a large bowl, mix all of the ingredients together. Taste for desired flavor, adding more salt, pepper, or dressing as needed.

Chill for 2 to 3 hours and then bring to room temperature before serving.

QUICK TIP

This pasta pairs well with wings and deviled eggs.

KEITH JR.'S SAUCE WINGS
SERVES ABOUT 6 TO 8

If time flies, then it must have wings. When my son, Keith, was a little boy he would hang out with me in the kitchen every night like clockwork. He was granted the hardest job of all by being my official taste tester.

The first time I attempted this recipe Keith was standing on duty, eyeing the platter as it moved closer to him. He was always there, someone I could count on in the kitchen and in my life. After his first bite he shouted, "Mom! I love your sauce wings," and just like that, Keith had named this dish.

These wings have matured in their flavor since that initial taste test, just as my son has. He is grown up and is still fun-loving, intelligent, and dependable as ever. There is so much truth around what we hear about time and how important it is to cherish the moments we have with loved ones. Savor your time and savor these sauce wings too!

¼ to ½ cup sweet chili sauce

2 tablespoons mild jerk seasoning

¼ cup honey

2 tablespoons orange zest

1 teaspoon ground ginger

1 teaspoon creole seasoning

1 teaspoon ground turmeric

1 teaspoon kosher salt

1 teaspoon all-purpose adobo seasoning

5 cloves garlic, minced

2 dozen chicken wing drumettes

Sliced scallions, for garnish (optional)

In a large bowl, whisk all of the ingredients except the chicken and scallions.

Reserve and refrigerate ½ cup of the marinade for basting.

Add the wings to the remaining marinade and toss to coat. Cover and refrigerate overnight or for at least 3 hours.

Let wings stand at room temperature for 45 minutes.

Preheat the oven to 350 F.

Line a rimmed baking sheet or 9x13-inch casserole dish with nonstick foil, arrange the wings, cover with foil, and bake for 25 minutes.

Remove the cover, turn the wings over, and brush with the reserved marinade.

Continue baking uncovered and brushing with marinade until wings are cooked and nicely browned, about 20 minutes more.

Turn the oven's broiler to high and let the wings broil for 2 to 3 minutes, keeping a close watch so that the wings do not burn.

Remove from the oven and let rest for 15 minutes before placing on a serving platter. Sprinkle with sliced scallions if desired.

CURRIED CHICKEN SALAD
SERVES 6 TO 8

1 cup chicken broth

1 cup water

1½ pounds boneless, skinless chicken breast halves, about ¾-inch thick

½ cup plain yogurt (light or nonfat)

3 tablespoons mayonnaise

1 teaspoon curry powder

1 cup seedless red grapes, halved

¼ cup red bell pepper, diced small

¼ cup celery, diced small

¼ cup chopped flat-leaf parsley or cilantro leaves

Salt and fresh-ground black pepper to taste

In a medium pot, bring the chicken broth and water to a boil. Add chicken to the broth, cover the pot, and simmer for about 10 minutes.

Turn the heat off and let the chicken stand in the cooking liquid, covered, for about 20 minutes to allow it to cook through.

Drain the chicken and let cool completely. Cut into ¼-inch cubes.

In a large bowl, add the yogurt, mayonnaise, and curry powder and mix well.

Fold in the diced chicken, grapes, bell pepper, celery, and parsley or cilantro and season to taste with salt and pepper.

Enjoy with crackers or green salad or serve it as a dip.

CLASSIC POTATO SALAD
SERVES ABOUT 8

5 russet potatoes, peeled and diced small

3 hard-boiled eggs, whites chopped small, yolks crushed

2 tablespoons white vinegar, more as needed

1 tablespoon granulated sugar, more as needed

1 teaspoon salt

½ sweet Vidalia onion, grated

Black pepper to taste

1 small carrot, peeled and grated

¼ cup red bell pepper, diced small

1 to 2 celery stalks, diced small

½ cup mayonnaise, more as needed

Celery leaves for garnish

In a medium pot, boil the diced potatoes to a medium texture. Drain well.

In a large bowl, toss the boiled potatoes with all of the ingredients and then add the mayonnaise and mix well. Avoid mashing the potatoes.

Mix thoroughly. Taste for desired flavor.

Transfer to serving bowl. Garnish with celery leaves. Cover and refrigerate.

Stir once more before serving to combine the flavors.

CRABBY PARTY PATTIES

SERVES 6

These crab cakes became a staple at our annual Christmas party as requested by our guests. They would ask if the crab cakes were on the menu when they received their invitations. The memory of a house filled with people decked in holiday attire, music, dancing, merriment, and of course *food* warms my heart! I hope you give this recipe a try and serve it at your next party.

¼ cup red bell pepper, finely chopped

¼ cup green onions, finely chopped

¼ cup parsley, finely chopped

1 large egg, beaten

¼ cup mayonnaise

1 tablespoon fresh-squeezed lemon juice

¼ teaspoon adobo all-purpose seasoning

½ teaspoon garlic powder

⅓ teaspoon cayenne pepper

12 ounces jumbo lump crabmeat

1 cup Italian bread crumbs, divided

4 to 5 tablespoons butter (for frying)

QUICK TIP

Jumbo lump and backfin crab meat are known for their bright white color and exquisite taste. Gently combined with each ingredient, you'll be sure to create beautiful crab cakes featuring whole pieces of unbroken meat.

In a bowl, combine the red pepper, green onions, parsley, egg, mayonnaise, lemon juice, adobo seasoning, garlic powder, and cayenne pepper.

Add the crab and ⅓ cup of the breadcrumbs. Mix very lightly to combine.

Portion into medium-sized balls and roll them in the remaining breadcrumbs. Flatten into cakes.

In a skillet, melt the butter over medium heat and fry the crab cakes for 3 to 4 minutes per side or until evenly browned on both sides. Drain on paper towels.

Serve warm or at room temperature.

just eat • sips

sips

KATHY'S PEACHY SANGRIA
MAKES 8 CUPS OR 2 QUARTS

I'm not much of an iced tea person, but when my "tea lady" and good friend, Kathryn, and I were having one of our tea conversations, she mentioned peaching it up into sangria. Following her tips, this sangria turned out to be quite the cocktail. Try it and have a peachy time at your next soiree.

4   cups boiling water

4   cups lukewarm water

8   peach tea sachets or enough loose leaf teas for 8 cups

1   orange, sliced

¼   cup peaches, sliced

¼   cup strawberries, sliced

¼   cup grapes, sliced

¼   cup apples, sliced

¼   cup raspberries, sliced

¼   cup mint leaves

1   bottle sweet wine, Riesling or Moscato (optional)

Superfine sugar, simple syrup, or honey to taste (optional)

QUICK TIP

To make simple syrup, in a saucepan add 1 cup water and 1 cup sugar or honey. Heat to a boil, stirring until the sugar or honey is completely dissolved. Cool completely. Pour into a dispenser and serve.

In a large pot, add the boiling water and steep the tea for 5 to 6 minutes or according to package directions.

Remove tea sachets or strain loose leaves.

Transfer tea to a pitcher and dilute with 4 cups lukewarm water. Chill overnight.

The next day, add the fruits, mint leaves, and wine. Sweeten to taste with superfine sugar, simple syrup, or honey. (If you prefer a "mocktail," replace the wine with club soda or nonalcoholic apple cider. You can also leave the sangria unsweetened and offer sweeteners on the side.)

Chill until cold and then serve.

GINGER REFRESHER (GINGER BEER)
SERVES 12

5 to 6 large ginger roots,
   peeled and chopped

1   gallon water, divided

½   cup sugar (possibly more to taste)

2   cinnamon sticks

5   whole cloves

Peel of one orange

1   teaspoon vanilla extract (optional)

Add the peeled and chopped ginger to a blender with 1 cup of water. Puree until finely chopped.

Pour the mixture into a large pot or deep bowl and add the remaining water with ½ cup sugar. Stir to dissolve.

Transfer the mixture to a large plastic or glass jar and add the cinnamon, cloves, and orange peel. Let set (ferment) for 7 days on the kitchen counter.

When ready, strain the mixture through a fine strainer into a large pot or bowl. Discard the chopped ginger and spices.

After straining, add the vanilla (if using) and more sugar to taste. If the flavor is too strong, add a little water to thin it out.

Refrigerate overnight. Serve over ice. Garnish with candied ginger.

WATERMELON SPLASH

SERVES 6-8

The first time I heard my mom say she was making this drink, I was not inclined to taste it. I am not fond of watermelon, but I do love ginger. I think that was her tricky way of making me taste it. I am glad I did because it's become one of my favorite drinks for the summer. I dress it up with a garnish of watermelon bits, candied ginger, and mint leaves. It makes an elegant drink and tastes delicious too.

6 to 8 cups watermelon, peeled, seeded, and cut into cubes

1 to 2½ cups water, more if needed

2 tablespoons honey (or more)

1 tablespoon fresh ginger, peeled and finely grated (from one small piece of ginger root)

Mint leaves (for garnish)

Candied ginger (for garnish)

Reserve a few cubes of watermelon for garnish.

In a blender, place the rest of the watermelon, water, honey, and grated ginger. Puree until smooth. Pour into a pitcher and stir well. Depending on the size of your blender, you may need to blend in batches and then stir the batches together in the pitcher.

Taste for sweetness and add more honey if desired.

Refrigerate until well chilled (at least 4 hours).

Fill glasses with ice cubes and divide the beverage among them. Using beverage picks, skewer one piece each of watermelon, candied ginger, and mint for garnish and serve.

TROPICAL GUAVA COCKTAIL
SERVES 1

1   can (11.5 ounces) guava nectar
4   ounces tropical fruit juice
4   ounces orange juice, pulp free

1 to 1½ ounces vodka (orange or plain)
Ice cubes

Add ice cubes to a small pitcher. Pour in all of the ingredients and stir well. Strain into an ice-filled cocktail glass and enjoy.

RENATE'S MARGARITA
SERVES 4

Salt to rim cocktail glasses
2   cups crushed ice
1   cup (8 ounces) tequila
1½ cups unsweetened
    margarita mix (Jose
    Cuervo recommended)

4   teaspoons fresh lime juice
    (about half of a large lime)
5   teaspoons superfine or
    granulated sugar
4   lime wedges, for garnish

Apply salt rims to cocktail glasses.

In a blender, add the ice cubes, tequila, margarita mix, lime juice, and sugar. Blend for 10 seconds or until smooth.

Taste for desired flavor.

Pour into cocktail glasses and garnish with lime wedges.

dips

SUNDRIED TOMATOES & OLIVES

SERVES 6-8

Guests always enjoy this dip at my gatherings. Not only is it quick and easy to prepare, it also pairs well with crackers, chips, baguettes, and more party favorites. It is also delicious when spread on pizza.

½ cup chopped sundried tomatoes (in olive oil)

1 can (6 ounces) of black olives, chopped

2 cloves of garlic, chopped

2 tablespoons olive oil, for mixing

Red pepper flakes to taste

Salt and pepper to taste

In a food processor, add the sundried tomatoes, olives, garlic, olive oil, and pulse until finely chopped. Add a pinch of red pepper flakes and salt to taste. Mix to combine. Taste for flavor of garlic, salt, and pepper. Add more if desired. If the mixture is too dry, add some more olive oil and mix well.

BRUSCHETTA TOPPING

SERVES 6-8

This refreshing dip can be put together quickly and will have your guests craving more. It pairs well with pita bites, crackers, baguettes, and nachos.

5 to 6 roma tomatoes, seeded and diced small

2 tablespoons red onion, diced small

1 tablespoon basil, chopped small

2 to 3 tablespoons olive oil

Salt and pepper to taste

Combine all of the ingredients, adding salt and pepper to taste. Allow to macerate for at least 5 minutes to enhance the flavors.

just eat • dips

PEPPER PECAN BRIE
SERVES 8-10

½ cup pecan halves

1 jalapeño pepper, stemmed, seeded, and finely chopped

¼ cup apricot preserves

1 4-inch round (8 ounce) Brie cheese with rind, room temperature

Heat oven to 375 F.

Coarsely chop the pecans.

In a small bowl, combine chopped jalapeño and preserves. Mix well to combine.

Cut Brie in half horizontally.

Place one half of Brie, cut side up, onto a foil-lined baking sheet. Spread half of the apricot mixture evenly and sprinkle half of the pecans on top of the Brie.

Top with the remaining half of Brie, placing the cut side up. Spread the remaining apricot mixture and sprinkle the remaining pecans on top.

Bake 8 to 10 minutes or until the Brie begins to soften. Remove from oven and let stand 5 minutes before serving.

Serve with warm slices of French baguette drizzled with olive oil.

PISTACHIO FIG BRIE
SERVES 8-10

1 4-inch (8 ounce) round Brie cheese with rind, room temperature

½ cup chopped pistachios

¼ cup fig jam

Zest of 1 orange

¼ cup sliced dried figs

Heat oven to 357 F.

Combine the chopped pistachios, fig jam, and orange zest.

Cut the Brie in half horizontally. Place one half cut side up on a nonstick foil-lined baking sheet. Spread half of the mixture and then sprinkle half of the chopped figs on top of the slice of Brie.

Place the other half of the Brie, cut side up, on the baking sheet and spread with the remaining mixture and top with remaining chopped figs.

Bake 8 to 10 minutes or until the Brie begins to soften. Remove from the oven and let stand 5 minutes before serving.

MANGO TANGO SALSA
SERVES 6-8

This salsa is a hit among my guests when eaten with butterflied shrimp, shrimp cocktail, or chips.

1 ripe yellow mango, (not too soft to the touch) peeled and diced medium

2 to 3 tablespoons red onion, chopped

½ cup cucumber, peeled, seeded, and diced small

1 to 2 teaspoons fresh lime juice

1 teaspoon fresh parsley or cilantro leaves, chopped

Salt and pepper to taste

Combine the diced mangoes, red onions, cucumber, lime juice, and parsley or cilantro leaves. Mix well and then season with salt and pepper to taste. Add extra lime juice if desired.

REN'S "HOLD THE CILANTRO" GUACAMOLE
MAKES ABOUT 2 CUPS

Despite the food connoisseur I am, I cannot tolerate the taste of cilantro, and I feel awful for discriminating against this herb, especially in guacamole! This is why it is difficult for me to enjoy guacamole whenever I dine out. So I always say, "Hold the cilantro, please!"

2 plum tomatoes

2 firm but ripe avocados

2 tablespoons red onion, minced

1 teaspoon garlic, minced

3 tablespoons fresh lime juice

Salt and pepper to taste

Quarter tomatoes, discard seeds, and dice small. Halve and pit the avocados. Scoop the avocado flesh into a bowl and mash with a fork, leaving some chunks. Stir in tomatoes, onion, and garlic. Mix well. Add the lime juice 1 tablespoon at a time. Add salt and pepper to taste. Taste for desired flavor. Enjoy with chips of your choice.

GEORGE'S LIMEADE (SWANK)

SERVES ABOUT 5 TO 10

To finish off this epicurist adventure, I find it appropriate to share a refreshing beverage to wash down all these great dishes. Limeade was my dad's everyday beverage to have with his lunch. He would pick one lime from our tree, squeeze the juice, and drop the rind into a tall glass filled with water and pure cane sugar stirred with ice cubes. Refreshing and healthy, this drink was perfect with his lunch. Relatives knew how much he loved his 'swank'. Limeade brings back a happy memory seeing my father making it and giving me a sip. Today, in my family, I make pitchers of it during the summer.

12 cups room-temperature water
Sugar to taste (1 to 1½ cups recommended)
Rind of 3 limes for garnish
6   large limes, juiced

Fill a large pitcher with water, add the sugar and rinds, and stir until the sugar dissolves. Add the lime juice, stir, and taste for desired sweetness. It should not be too sweet. Chill or pour into glasses filled with ice cubes and enjoy.

just eat

just eat • *this & that*

this & that

KITCHEN TIPS

Cleaning Poultry

Growing up in South America, we used a particular method to clean poultry before cooking it. I realize cleaning raw meat has become controversial, but I still use this method and believe it is worthwhile. The acids tenderize the meat and allow marinades to infuse the meat more thoroughly. Wash the meat with a solution of warm water, vinegar, and lemon or lime juice. If using fresh lemons or limes, add the rinds to the water. Soak the meat for about 12 to 15 minutes (but no longer) and then give it a good rinse under running water. Drain well and pat dry with paper towels. Then marinate or cook.

Cleaning the Garbage Disposal

Keep your kitchen garbage disposal smelling fresh and free from bacteria by dropping pieces of lemon or lime rinds down and then turning the disposal on with running water. Baking soda and vinegar are good ingredients too.

Sharpening the Garbage Disposal Blades

Use ice cubes or discarded egg shells to keep garbage disposal blades sharpened. Also make sure the water is running while the disposal is on.

Working with Onions

Fresh lemon juice will remove onion scent from hands.

Keeping Vegetables Fresh

For a longer shelf life, wrap cucumbers, peppers, eggplants, and similar vegetables with paper towels and then place them in plastic bags and store in the refrigerator.

Baking Bread

You will get a finer texture when you use milk as your liquid. Water makes coarser bread.

Icing a Cake

The icing will remain where you put it if you sprinkle the cake with powdered sugar first.

MEASUREMENTS

Conversions

A pinch..⅓ tsp

3 teaspoons...................................1 tbsp

4 tablespoons.............................¼ cup

8 tablespoons.............................½ cup

12 tablespoons...........................¾ cup

16 tablespoons ....1 cup

2 cups ....1 pint

4 cups...1 quart

4 quarts.......................................1 gallon

16 ounces..................................1 pound

32 ounces...................................1 quart

1 liquid ounce...........................2 tbsps

8 liquid ounces.............................1 cup

Cutting Measurements in Half

If you want to make fewer servings of a recipe, these conversions will prove helpful.

1 cup ....½ cup

¾ cup ....6 tbsps

⅔ cup ....⅓ cup

½ cup ....¼ cup

⅓ cup ....2 tbsps + 2 tsps

¼ cup ....2 tbsps

3 tbsps........................ 1 tbsp + 1½ tsps

2 tablespoons.............................1 tbsp

1 tablespoon..............................1½ tsps

PANTRY BASICS

I'm often asked what are great items to stock a pantry, and I'd say, "It depends on what you like." Although everyone's pantry is different, there are some basic items you should always have. Below are some of my pantry staples that help me put together meals easily. But only you can determine the essentials based on the preferences of your family. The idea is to make sure you have enough proteins and sturdy vegetables to pull together several satisfying meals, along with flavorful condiments and seasonings to keep things interesting (even on a school night). Don't forget refrigerated items such as milk, eggs, cheese, butter, bell peppers, celery, onions, green onions, and carrots.

Packaged and Canned Foods
Beans (canned/dry)
Broth (vegetable/beef/chicken)
Canned diced tomatoes
Canned fruit
Canned healthy tuna and chicken
Canned mushrooms
Canned olives (pitted, whole, and sliced)
Canned soups (variety)
Canned tomato sauce
Couscous
Gravies
Jarred pasta sauce
Milk (evaporated and sweetened condensed)
Orzo
Pastas
Powdered milk
Rice
Tomato paste

Staples
Baker's chocolate
Baking powder
Baking soda

Staples (continued)
Barbeque sauce
Bread crumbs (plain or seasoned)
Cake flour
Chocolate chips
Cornmeal
Cornstarch
Crackers
Dijon mustard
Dutch cocoa powder
Flour
Ghee (clarified butter)
Gluten-free flour
Ground espresso
Ground flaxseed meal
Honey
Jams (apricot, fig, raspberry, and/or strawberry)
Ketchup
Kosher salt
Lemon juice
Maple syrup
Mayonnaise
Nonstick cooking spray
Nuts (walnuts, pecans, sliced almonds, and/or chopped pistachios)

just eat • this & that

Staples (continued)

Oatmeal
Oil (olive, coconut, canola,
   and/or vegetable)
Orange marmalade
Pancake baking mix
Pancake syrup
Peanut butter
Salad dressing
Sugar (brown, granulated,
   coconut, and confectioners)
Vegetable shortening
Vinegar
Tapioca
Vermicelli
Raisins
Cranberries (dried)
Pitted dates
Figs (dried)

Spices and Seasonings

Almond extract
Basil
Bay leaves
Black pepper
Bouillon cubes (beef, chicken,
   and/or vegetable)
Chili powder
Cinnamon sticks
Coriander
Crushed red pepper
Curry powder
Garlic powder

Goya adobo all-purpose seasoning
Ground cardamom
Ground cinnamon
Ground cloves
Ground ginger
Ground nutmeg
Herbes de Provence
Onion powder
Parsley
Rose water
Rosemary
Sage
Salt
Soy sauce
Sweet paprika
Tarragon
Thyme
Tony Chachere's creole seasoning
Turmeric
Vanilla bean
Vanilla extract
Whole allspice
Whole cloves
Worcestershire sauce
Yeast

just eat

AFTERWORD

I grew up hearing my parents say, "Early to bed, early to rise makes us healthy, wealthy, and wise." As a grown up, I processed that saying and found the meaning to be true. With good sleep, we allow our minds to rest and our bodies to heal. As we rise early, our work becomes our wealth. Creating this circle of balance is essential in the journey to happiness.

I hope I have inspired you to cook, create, and try new things that are not only noteworthy tastewise but also nourishing. As I look back on my upbringing and the lifestyle of my grandparents, parents, and now my own, I realize we were eating healthy and just didn't know it. We didn't focus on how nutritious our meals were; we just enjoyed food and our days cooking and eating delicious foods made with the best ingredients. Both of my grandmothers were very active working ladies. They stayed healthy and lived long and cheerful lives. Doctor visits were a rarity. One of my grandmothers passed away at 101 years old. She was still reading the daily newspaper, drinking coffee before bed, and making trips to the market.

These recipes will lead you to your own robust and happy life! Enjoy.

just eat

ACKNOWLEDGMENTS

So many people—new friends, clients, people who tasted my cooking for the first time, and old friends and family—prompted me and insisted I put my recipes in a cookbook. "I want to learn to cook these types of food," they'd say. I would like to thank them for that.

Thank you to my mother, Shelia, who introduced me to the joy of cooking; my father, George, for graciously eating whatever I served him and always paying a compliment no matter the taste; Keith Moore, my bluntly honest taste tester and husband for giving me the truth always; my picky eater son, Keith Jr., for pushing my limits to please your palette; my daughter, Kellieann, for your unusual and exotic tastes that challenged me to try new recipes; and my brother, Fenton Khan, for sharing the love of cooking with me through recipe tips and precious time we spend together cooking. Thank you!

I never thought I would be able to create a cookbook because it seemed like a *lot* of work, and I didn't know where and how to begin since my cooking ideas come naturally and mostly without measurement or structure. It started out with a concept in my head to a manuscript. It was tough getting started, and my rough draft was very rough. I almost gave up. Then as people continued to ask me when I was going to write a cookbook because they wanted it, I felt compelled to get it done. Knowing that people were eager to cook what I cooked motivated me to finish this project.

For me, writing is not easy when the room isn't quiet. I'd like to thank Kim Barker, my writing consort who helped me to bring this book to life by providing the Zen and quietness I needed, especially when I had a short deadline to submit my manuscript.

I thank my dear friend Denise Peters who jump-started me with one single interview to take these recipes from my head and put them on paper. And when I felt overwhelmed, she made girls night out fun to help me regroup.

I am very thankful to my sweet friend Kathryn Isaacs, who continuously checked in with me to offer support, even if it meant just keeping me company.

Thanks to the SPARKlers at SPARK Publications who worked with me and helped me very much. Special thanks to Fabi Preslar, the ever-patient chief SPARKler who took the pressure off me and encouraged me to finish what she called "this amazing book."

Special thanks to my photographer Mark Santo for making each moment captured fun and whose talents are unmatched by any other.

Love and thanks to everyone from the bottom of my heart.

ABOUT THE AUTHOR

Renate Moore is the founder and owner of LadyRen's Bakery & Books, a gourmet bakery and bookshop. Her clientele includes people who are passionate about living their best lives. Her passions are cooking and writing. Through them, she educates and shares her expertise in making delicious yet healthy food using all-natural ingredients, promotes literacy and encourages reading, and promotes books to stimulate the mind.

Renate has also published two bestselling children's books, *A Frog in Grandma's Cup* and *Mystery Picnic on Stone Mountain.* Her third book, *Just Eat,* is a journey of her life surrounded by food and family and the sweet memories they've created.

She is a wife, mother, author, entrepreneur, gourmet baker, human and animal rights activist, and literacy advocate who hopes to leave a legacy of fearless achievement and girl power! Her accomplishments include being named VIP Woman of the Year by the National Association of Professional Women (NAPW) for excellence, leadership, and commitment to the profession while encouraging the achievement of professional women. She was also recognized by Continental Who's Who for professional and executive excellence.

Connect with Renate on social media.

ladyrensbb

renate.moore

Subscribe to Renate's blog, sign up for her newsletter, or order additional books.
www.ladyrens.com

Contact Renate for speaking engagements on living your best life.
info@ladyrens.com

CPSIA information can be obtained
at www.ICGtesting.com
Printed in the USA
JSHW051137140822
29219JS00002B/2